Indigenous Writers of India
Introduction and Contributions

Details of the Forthcoming Volumes

Vol. II : Eastern India	—	West Bengal, Orissa, Jharkhand, Bihar
Vol. III : South India	—	Andhra Pradesh, Karnataka, Kerala, Tamil Nadu
Vol. IV : Western and Central India	—	Gujarat, Rajasthan, Maharashtra, Goa, Jammu and Kashmir, Madhya Pradesh and Chattishgarh

Ramnika Foundation

Ramnika Foundation, a non-political, non-commercial and absolutely secular organisation, works for bringing an equalitarian change in society through empowering the marginalised and oppressed communities like the tribals, dalits, minorities and women working in the social sector for the last many years, the Foundation has the distinction of piloting and pioneering many successful initiatives, both at the ideological and material levels.

The Foundation embodies efforts and struggles, hopes and aspirations of the common people for developing a dynamic and responsive civil society, a society which ensures human rights and dignity, health and education to the marginalised millions.

About the Editor

Ramnika Gupta, former member of Bihar Vidhan Sabha, is presently President of Ramnika Foundation. Also, she is editor of a Hindi quarterly journal *Yudha Rat Aam Aadmi,* and Joint Secretary of Democratic Writers Association (Bihar-Jharkhand Chapter) as well as Member of National Council of Democratic Writers Association. She is a well-known Hindi poetess and novelist and has to her credit many collections of poems, short stories, novels and essays. She has bagged several awards for her literary achievements and social service.

INDIGENOUS WRITERS OF INDIA

Introduction and Contributions

Volume I : North-East India

Editor

Ramnika Gupta

Published for
RAMNIKA FOUNDATION
by
CONCEPT PUBLISHING COMPANY, NEW DELHI-110059

ISBN 81-8069-299-X (Series)
ISBN 81-8069-300-7 (Vol. I)

First Published 2006

Published and Printed by
Ashok Kumar Mittal
Concept Publishing Company
A/15-16, Commercial Block, Mohan Garden
New Delhi-110059 (INDIA)

Phones : 25351460, 25351794
Fax : 091-11-25357103
Email : publishing@conceptpub.com

Dedicated to the Indigenous Writers'
of the Invisible India

Introduction

This is a book about Invisible India. With this publication, we have tried to peel back the dark curtains around the people and lands of the North-East and offered our readers a glimpse of the multi-hued cultural panorama of this diverse collection of states and communities.

This bibliography, published side-by-side in Hindi and English, marks for the first time that the Tribal writers of the North-Eastern states of India have been recognized and brought together in a single volume. This is a landmark achievement, that will help the various writers of the North-East for their impressive work and which will also contribute greatly to the enrichment of Indian language and literature.

The writers included in this volume represent the seven states and more than fifteen languages which comprise the land and tribal communities of North-East India. It is a land of cultural diversities and rich linguistic and social history, but a land whose people are too often neglected by the "mainstream" Indian national culture, so much so that we have come to think of the North-East itself as a kind of "invisible India." Many Indian citizens in the North-East face looks of incomprehension when they travel to other parts of the country and are even sometimes asked, "Are you Indian?" The purpose of this volume is to bring the richness of this area's history and present it to light. In bringing these writers and their achievements together in a single volume, we hope to begin a much-needed dialogue between the creative communities of the North-East and the rest of the country, which for too long has remained ignorant of the literary, linguistic, and cultural achievements of various tribal communities in the North-East. And we hope to bring to the people of the North-East, a kind of exposure and national recognition that they have been denied until now.

The languages of the North-East are ancient, but they survived as oral languages until the arrival of Christian missionaries in the eighteenth and nineteenth centuries. Indeed the Lepcha language of Sikkim is believed to be even older than Sanskrit, but a written script was not created until Reverend William Start started a school for Lepcha language and culture in 1841. One interesting folk tale tells the story of how the spirits presented a script to the Mizo people on a piece of leather in ancient times, but due to negligence, it was eaten up by a dog. Thus the Mizos had to wait until 1894, when Reverends F.W. Savage and J.H. Lawrence created a script based to represent the vowel sounds of the language of communication between hunters, known as the Huntarian system in Mizoram. A great scholar Ram Das Boro is of opinion that Boro language was so rich that several of its aspects are considered to be the source of the Indian languages. It is a proven fact that the Boros came to India before the Aryans.

Madhu Ram Boro says that during the regime of the Boro kings, Devdhai script was in vogue. This script is engraved on the remnants of the Royal Gate at Deemapur.

Hence Bodos had a written script (which was subsequently lost) when they were rulers of this area during the Ahom Dynasty, it too was not recipient again of a written alphabet until 1895 when Reverend J.D. Anderson created the first script and grammar. Khasi emerged as a written language under the direction of a Welshman named Thomas Jones between 1810 and 1849 in Meghalaya, and was later improved upon and codified by Khasi intellectuals Jeebon Roy and Radhon Singh Berry. The achievements of all of these languages in creating a rich body of literature in only the last 100-150 years are therefore extremely impressive. One tribal writer refers to the development of a canon of Boro literature in the space of only fifty years like a "galloping horse". While it should be said that the development of all the languages of the North-East has been certainly uneven, that some languages have achieved greater success than others in the world of literature. For example with six Padmashree awards given to Mizo writers including two women, and several writers in Assam including Boro, Karbi and other tribal writers. It is also important to point out that tribal writers of all the languages and cultures and they are working hard towards that goal.

The tribal writers of the North-East do not simply write. They are linguistic, dealing with social and cultural activists and fighting for the life of their own native tongues. The writers in these pages have not only written creative literature, but have also codified grammars of their native languages. They have also produced histories of their communities stretching beyond recorded nationalist histories that examine prehistoric period, so that they may know the roots of their culture, community, and language. They have also written educational books for children and adult students, and translated important national and international works of literature and history into their local languages. In particular, the Boros, without any government assistance, have translated so many of the world's "classics," such as Shakespeare, Tagore, and the Hindu epics, into the Boro language. That they have succeeded in making Boro a language fit to be the principal medium of education in primary and secondary schools in some parts of Assam. Even a quick look at the entries included in this bibliography will impress the reader with the incredible literary and linguistic achievements of these tribal writers in just the last sixty years since Independence and creation of the North-East states.

Each individual entry of the more than ninety writers included in this volume offers more than just personal data and a list of publications. Every entry is also a window into the writers' culture, and the various ways that each of them has used literature to preserve and promote their own Languages and community Identities.

Though we have made our best efforts, we cannot claim that this volume represents all of the tribal writers of the North-East. We faced many hurdles due to lack of communication, the geographical distance and spread of these writers, as well as due to their sheer number. A second, and even more complete, volume is already being planned. But we hope that this book will serve only as a starting point for interested readers and students of Indian literature and culture to explore the rich collection of authors in the North-East. Any survey of Indian literature and culture would be incomplete without them.

Three years ago when I made up my mind to prepare and publish this bibliography of the North-Eastern tribal writers, the enormity of labour involved in it stood in the way. One of the major challenges was to collect information about the writers. Dr. L.T. Liana Khiangte and Darchhawna from Mizoram, Bijoya Sawian from Meghalaya and Mangal Sing Hazowary from Assam came to our rescue and arranged both addresses of the writers and materials in their respect. I owe a debt of gratitude to each of them. Dr. Khiangte, Darchhawna (Mizo) and Bijoya Sawian (Khasi), Mangal Sing Hazowary (Bodo) and Theso Cropy (Karbi) took pains for us to transcribe the names of the writers accurately in Hindi.

It was Shri Prakash of kritika, Ranchi, who made it possible to contact writers by E-mail, telephone or by visiting places personaly where neccessary to get the Biodata required, for the book. I must thank him for this.

Once the requisite information and materials began to pour in, the real problem was to incorporate them in presentabe write-ups. I wish to acknowledge my very great obligations to Aquil Quais who helped me on this front right from the beginning. Most of the write-ups of this bibliography have been prepared by him. It is no exaggeration to say that without his help, this book could not have been possible. Later on Ms. Ginger from U.S. joined the project and made necessary corrections. When she left India, Ms. Laura Brueck from U.S. (who is doing Ph.D. on Hindi Dalit writers) joined the team. She made significant contribution in making the prose of the book (English version) more acceptable to the readers at large. I express my hearty appreciation to each of them for their kind and helpful association.

I am also indebted to Mr. Dinesh, Mr. Rakesh, Mr. Ram Kuresh and others who helped in composing the matter of the bibliography patiently for months together. I must mention with special reference to Mr. Hare Prakash Upadhyaya who saw the proofs with special care and helped significantly in editing the stuff of the book in the final stage.

This volume of the bibliography is the first of a series of publications that we intend to bring out in course of time. While we intend to publish an enlarged edition of this first volume, many more volumes focusing on tribal writers from other parts of the country will be brought out. The next volume will be focused on eastern states viz., Orissa, Jharkhand, West Bengal and Bihar, southern states comprising Tamil Nadu, Andhra Pradesh, Karnataka, Kerala and western states of Maharashtra, Gujarat, Goa and Rajasthan, central states of Madhya Pradesh and Chhattisgarh and the remaining states viz. Uttaranchal, Himachal Pradesh, Jammu & Kashmir, Punjab and Delhi. Though tribals inhabiting all parts of the country have suffered and neglected, the north-eastern tribals are the worst sufferers. For this very reason, this first volume of the bibliography is focused on them. It is regretted that we could not include the writers of Sikkim for lack of communication. Lepcha writers living in West Bengal have found a place in it.

I take great pleasure to commend this book to the readers and scholars. Suggestions to improve this volume and the other ones to come in the series are welcome.

Ramnika Gupta

CONTENTS

Manipur

Paite/Tangkhul

Meghalaya

Khasi

Mizoram

Mizo

Nagaland
Tenydie

Tripura
Kokborok

Writers of Sikkim Living in West Bengal

Lepcha and Nepali

Arunachal Pradesh

Adi/Apatani

BANI DANGGEN

Personal

Bani Danggen was born in Palling village in the Upper Siang District of Arunachal Pradesh. In his childhood he became an A. L. C. load carrier, but he was so young that he could barely manage to carry anything, so he was assigned to cook the A.L.C. Babu's food. After a year he was appointed as a Dak Kunner.

In 1963, he began his political career as a student when he became secretary of Adi Branch Student Union. In 1964, he won first prize in an extemporary speech competition at the All North-Eastern Students Meet in Guwahati. In 1976, he began his political career and became a member of the District Congress Committee. Then, in the 1977 elections, he joined hands with the Shri Bakin Partin Peoples' Party of Arunachal (P.P.A.) and in the same year he was elected as District Vice President. He became the Vice President of the state unit of the Janata Dal in 1993, and in the same year he also became the Chairman of the Teachers' Cell. In 1995, he joined the Arunachal Development Council as a member.

Education

Bani Danggen first studied in the Karko Inter-village School. In 1957, he joined Pani Khowa Baptist Mission School. Within one and a half years he was promoted to class five. He joined Dumduma High School in 1959. In 1960, he was back at Along High School (West Siang District, Arunachal Pradesh). He achieved second position in his Matric final in NEFA (Now Arunachal Pradesh), and for this he was awarded an Advisers prize. After higher secondary school, he went on to study in J.N. College at Pasighat and St. Stephen's College of Delhi University. He also obtained orange nursing training in Japan. In 1965, Danggen won all nine literary prizes in the college week of J.N. College, Pasighat, East Siang District (A.P.).

Contributions

Bani Daggen is a well-known expert in the system of tribal affairs. A widely travelled person, he has engaged primarily in writing and social work. His two books include **Kebang** and **The Book of Conversation**. **Kebang** is a study of three aspects regarding a unique indigenous political institution of Adi society. In this book he looks at the historical and mythological background of the Kebang system, its contemporary practice and the **Bogun-Bokang**, the highest political institution of the **Adis society**.

Selected Published Works

Kebang—2003, **The Book of Conversation**—2003.

Contact Information

Bani Danggen
Gegi Shopping Complex
Tinali Itanagar
Pin : 110024
Telephone : 0360-2291910

MAMANG DAI

Personal

Mamang Dai was born on February 23,1957 at Pasighat, East Siang District, in Arunachal Pradesh. Her father's name is (retd.) Chief Secretary Matin Dai and her mother's name is Odi Dai. She was Selected to the IAS/IFS, 1979. Subsequently she left the service to pursue a career in journalism. She was appointed to the post of Programme Officer with World Wide Fund for Nature (WWF), Itanagar Office, during the first year of its establishment in the State. She worked in this capacity with the Bio-diversity Hotspots Conservation programme in the field of research, survey and protection of the Flora and Fauna of the eastern Himalayas. She was appointed adviser (Culture & Publicity) for the Donyi-Polo Mission, a voluntary organisation, and was involved with numerous programmes in the school for the Hearing Impaired, Itanagar.

Education

Mamang Dai did her schooling at Boarding school in Pine Mount School, Shillong, Meghalaya. She did her B.A. in **English Literature** from Guahati University Assam.

Contribution

Mamang is a Poetess, Story writer and a Journalist. She has written two books of poetry and one book in prose about Arunachal Pradesh. According to her, **as far as I can remember I was always writing stories, poems, essays, in school and at home. I also read every book I could find especially during the school holidays when my father was posted in remote outposts. Even now I keep notebooks and journals.**

She is Accredited journalist to the government of Arunachal Pradesh. Reporter for the **Sentinel** and **Telegraph** newspapers since 1992; and currently writing for **Open Forum in the Statesman,**

Kolkata, and for **Guest column in The Telegraph**, Guwahati. She is also affiliated to **All India Radio** and **Door Darshan (DDK)**, Itanagar, covering news programmes and interviews since **DDK** was inaugurated in the state in 1996.

Currently she is the President, Arunachal Pradesh Union of Working Journalists (APUWJ) and former Secretary, Itanagar Press Club. She is Vice-President of the North East Writers' Forum (NEWF), an organisation of writers/poets/essayists representing all the States of the North-East, including Sikkim, dedicated to the cause of promoting the literature of North East India.

She received the State's first **Annual Verrier Elwin prize** in the field of publication and print media. on her book **Arunachal Pradesh The Hidden Land.**

Selected Published Works

Arunachal Pradesh The Hidden Land, River Poems, Mountain Harvest The Food of Arunachal Pradesh.

Contact Information

Mamang Dai
Gute-Gamroh, C- Sector, Itanagar : 791111,
Itanagar (Arunachal Pradesh)
Telephone : 91- 0360-2212694.
E-mail : mamangdai@hotmail.com

N.N. OSIK

Personal

N. N. Osik was born on April 28, 1961 in Padu village in the upper Siang District of Arunachal Pradesh. He is a member of the Abor tribe. After his post graduation he worked as a school teacher 1983-84. He then became a District Research Officer. In 1985 Osik joined the Arunachal Pradesh Civil Services as an Extra Assistant Commissioner. He presently works as the Director of Civil Supplies for the Government of Arunachal Pradesh.

Education

Osik received his primary education at his village school in Pedu. He passed his matriculation from Government Higher Secondary School, Meob, in 1977. He joined St. Edmunds College, Shillong, for graduation and was awarded History Honours in 1981. He received his post-graduation from North East Hill University, Shillong, in 1983. While serving in different capacities in Arunachal Government he obtained a Doctorate in Philosophy in 1991 from Dibrugarh University.

Contribution

Osik started writing at a very early age. His first poem **Bidai Prarthana** was published in the Assamese journal *Deepak*. He has written articles and short stories for different magazines. **Myths Legends And Folktales Of Arunachal Pradesh** (2002) is a commendable contribution. He has written a **History of Arunachal Pradesh** and a book on the songs, dances, and holy places of his state.

Selected Published Works

Song and Dances of Arunachal Pradesh (Directorate of Art and Culture, Naharlagun)—2002. **Myths, Legends and Folk Tales of Arunachal Pradesh** (Directorate of Art and Culture, Naharlagun)—

2002, **Nibo–Robo** (A Myth of Abo Tani group of Arunachal Pradesh) Directorate of Art and Culture, Naharlagun—2002, **Holy Places of Arunachal Pradesh**, (Directorate of Art and Culture, Naharlagun)—2002, **Modern History of Arunachal Pradesh** (Himalayan Publishers, New Delhi, Itanagar)—2000, **A Brief History of Arunachal Pradesh** (Omsons Publications, New Delhi)—1993, **British Relations with Adis** (Omsons Publications, New Delhi)—1991.

TAKHE KANI

Personal

Takhe Kani was born on April 12, 1964 in a tribal family in Arunachal Pradesh. He is an essayist who writes primarily research-oriented articles on anthropological topics. He has also compiled several folk stories. Kani is presently in government service.

Education

Takhe Kani is a graduate.

Contribution

Kani's contribution is considerable. His writings provide a window on the Apatani tribal community of Arunachal Pradesh in all aspects: socio-religious ceremonies and rituals, festivals, mythology, social customs and laws, history, and art and crafts. In addition, Kani has written a book of Apatani grammar and compiled an **English-Apatani** Dictionary. An author of over a dozen books, Kani has published articles in various magazines and newspapers in Arunachal Pradesh. However, many of his essays have yet to appear in a book form.

In addition to the above books, he has contributed more than 100 research papers to seminars, newspapers, journals etc.

Selected Published Works

Current Affair of North-East India—2002, General Studies on North-East India with Special Reference to Arunachal Pradesh—(2001), Hand Book of North-East India including Sikkim—1999, Apatani Genesis of Man—1997, Socio-Religious Ceremonies of the Apatani—1996, English-Apatani Dictionary—1995, Agricultural Festival of Arunachal Pradesh—1995, Charung Hulu : A Ritual Text of the Apatani—1994, The Advancing Apatani of Arunachal Pradesh (A.P.)—1993,

G.K on Fact figures of North-East States—1989, The Apatani Grammar—1924.

Contact Information

Takhe Kani
Research Officer,
Economic Affairs, Development of Finance,
Government of Arunachal Pradesh

42, Itanagar, Papumpare,
Arunachal Pradesh-791111
Telephone : 0368-2212070

TAGANG TAKI

Personal

Tagang Taki was born in a small village in Arunachal Pradesh on February 10, 1942. He is a political activist and a social worker.

Education

Taki has a Masters degree in History from Gauhati University, Assam.

Contribution

Taki has written several books in English as well as in the Adi language. Taki has also written several novels, dramas, and poems in Assamese and Adi, which are unpublished. He is currently compiling an **English-Adi Dictionary**.

Selected Published Works

Nibo Aru Robor Sadhu (an Adi Legend, in Assamese)—1998, **Adi English Word Book**—1998, **Border Eme** (drama, in Adi and Assamese)—1965, **Adi Sadhu** (folktales, in Assamese)—1964, **Appeal to the NEFA Students**—1959, **Adi Assamese Word Book**—1959.

Contacted Information

Tagang Taki
Post : Pangin,
District : East Siang
Pin : 791102
(Arunachal Pradesh)
Telephone : 03793-2222335

YESHE DORJEE THONGCHI

Personal

Yeshe Dorjee Thongchi was born in May, 1952 in a remote tribal village named Zhigang in Arunachal Pradesh. He belongs to the Sherdukpen tribe, whose population is around four thousand. His father was the late Phuntso Thongchi and his mother is Rinchin Chojom. Yeshe lost his father when he was about five years old. Consequently, he and his seven brothers and sisters grew up in poverty. After completing his education, he entered the Arunachal Pradesh Civil Service and was later elevated to the Indian Administrative Service.

Education

Thongchi's schooling began at Government Primary School, Jigaon. He was later educated at Government Higher Secondary School in Bomdila; Cotton College, Guwahati; and finally, at Gauhati University. Thongchi completed his post-graduation in Arts from Gauhati University. He gives credit to the free education system in Arunachal Pradesh for enabling him to receive education despite living a life of extreme poverty.

Contribution

A prose writer, Thongchi writes fiction, drama and essays in Assamese and English. Three of his novels have been published : **Sonam** (1981), **Lingjhik** (1982), and **Maun Oudh Kukhar Hriday** (2001). **Sonam** is based on the life of the nomadic Brokpas, a shepherd tribe of Himalayan region that practises **Polyandry. Lingjhik,** on the other hand is based on experiences of his own tribe. Thongchi's other important works include **Kamang Himantar Hadu,** a collection of folk tales published in 1972, and **Paper Pukhuri,** a collection of short stories published in 2000. His short stories have been translated into Hindi. The writer feels that **After Lummer Dai and myself there is a vacuum in creative writing in Arunachal Pradesh, as our younger** generation did not receive any patronage from Hindi writers and editors of literary magazines. He feels that This has happened in spite of the fact that Hindi is now taught in schools and has replaced Assamese as the *lingua franca* in my state, where there is no common language amongst the approximately thirty tribes speaking about ninety dialects.

He is a recipient of the **Harihar Choudhary Award** (1970) and the **Bishnu Rawa Award** (2002) from the Assam Sahitya Sabha. He is also a recipient of the **Phulchand Khandelwal Sangheti Bata Award** from the Golaghat Sahitya Sabha.

Selected Published Works

Maun Oudh Kukhar Hriday (novel)—2001, **Paper Pukhuri** (short stories)—2000, **Lingjhik** (novel)—1982, **Sonam** (novel)—1981, **Kameng Himantar Hadu** (folk tales)—1972.

Contact Information

Yeshe Dorjee Thongchi
Secretariate
Arunachal Pradesh
Government
Itanagar
(Arunachal Pradesh)
Telephone : 0360-2211799 (R)

Assam

Boro/Garo/Karbi/Rabha/ Santali/Tiwa

ANIL KUMAR BORO

Personal

Anil Kumar Boro was born on December 9, 1961 in the Bodo Tribe of Assam. Presently he works as a teacher in the department of Folklore Research in Guahati University. He is convenor of North-East regional committee of All India Tribal Literary Forum and also a member of its central committee at the national level.

Education

He did M.A. in English from the University of Gauahati and Ph.D. in the folklore of the Bodos.

Contribution

Anil Boro is a Bodo poet, critic and novelist. He writes in Bodo, Assamese, and English.

Selected Published Works

Folk Literature of the Bodos (an introduction), **Adhunik Bodo Sahitya** (in Assamese). In addition to these books, he has written two collections of poems and two collections of critical analysis on Bodos.

Contact Information

Anil Kumar Boro
Guwahati
Po : Bassistha,
Distt. : Kamrup-781029 (Assam)
Telephone : 0361-2300327 (R)

BHUPEN NARZAREE

Personal

Bhupen Narzaree was born on August 1, 1960 in the Bodo Tribe of Dahalpara village in Bongaigaon, Assam. He works in Guahati University, Assam as a lecturer in the Department of M.I.L. (Bodo). He has attended and actively participated twice in international seminars, four times in national-level seminars and 20 times in regional seminar within the state. He also participated at least 15 times in workshops organised by C.I.L. Mysore, Sahitya Akademi, N.B.T. and ABILAC, Guwahati.

He is also a member of Guahati University for the graduate and post-graduate courses, Dibrugarh University, Assam Higher Secondary Council and SEBA, Guwahati, Assam. For some time he worked as a lecturer in Bijni College. He has been working in M.I.L. Department of Gauhati University since March 30, 1988.

Education

He had his primary education in his village school. Subsequently, he was admitted to Bijni Bandhav High School, located at Bijni Nagar. He did his matriculation from this school in 1976 and then joined Bijni College, Bijni Nagar. He did B.A.(Honours) there in 1981. In 1983 he did M.A. in Bodo literature from Gauhati University.

Contribution

Mr. Narzaree is a Bodo poet, novelist, short story writer and essayist. He writes in Bodo, Assamese, Bengali and English. He has written nine books and published more than 50 papers. More than 100 articles of Mr. Narzaree are published in various journals and magazines in Assamese, Bodo, Bengali and English.

He has actively participated in the text preparation workshop as per the guidelines of the National Educational Policy organised by SCERT (Assam) and Sarba Siksha Abhzan Mission (Assam).

Selected Published Works

Sungdo Soloni Mala (Edited)—2003, **Laisini Bikhayao Indra Malati**—2003, **Rangina Sangina Thunlai** (Edited)—2003, **Gaodang**—2003, **Miri Sikhla** (Edited)—2003, **Jiuni Lamayao** (Edited)—2002, **Mithingani Aijw Sakuntala**—2002, **Khardeni Jiu**—2002, **Sujunai Bijab** (Edited)—1997, **Mansi Jagra Mwsa**—1997, **Nursery Rhymes** (In Bodo)—1995, **Maisaguni Radab**—1995, **Angni Mwjang Mwnnaini Dairy**—1995, **Maharaja Ashok**—1994.

Contact Information

Bhupen Narzaree (Sr. Lecturer),
Deptt. of M. I. L., Guahati University,
Guwahati-781014 (Assam)
Telephone : 0361-2572429

BROJENDRA KUMAR BRAHMA

Personal

Brojendra Kumar Brahma was born on June 1, 1943 in Batabari village of Kokrajhar district. His father was Sri Dandaram Brahma, a cultivator, and his mother was Endab Brahma, a housewife. From 1970 to 2001 he was the headmaster of Banargaon High School. He now lives in Bagansali village under the Kokrajhar municipality board. He has been involved with several additional organizations since the completion of his education in 1968.

Education

Brahma matriculated from Sakti Ashram Vocational High School in 1959. He is a graduate of St. Edmunds College, Shillong, and passed B.T. in 1977 from Government B.T. College, Goalpara.

Contribution

Brahma's appreciation of literature developed while he was a high school student. His first book of poetry, **Okhrang Gongse Nanggou,** was published in 1975. Since then six books have been published, three of critical prose and three of poetry. Several of his articles and poems are currently being published as books.

Brahma has been closely associated with various Bodo literary organizations and is serving a three year term as president of the Bodo Sahitya Sabha. In addition, he has held important positions in the Bodo Sahitya Sabha and the Bodo Writers Academy. He was Chairman, Editorial Board, THE BODO (publication by the BSS) (1993-1995), and also headed the Award Selection Sub-Committee, BSS, (1996-2002).

Selected Published Works

Okhrang Gongse Nanggou (collection of poems)—1975-2003, **Ang**

Fwifingwn (collection of poems)—1994-2003, **Sanmwkhangari Bibar Jananwi** (collection of poems)—1994-2003, **Thunlai Arw Sansri** (criticism)—1986-2000, **Nwjwr Arw Sansri** (criticism)—1994, **Raithaimala** (criticism)—1992.

Contact Information

Brojendra Kumar Brahma
7/62, Bagansali, W/7,
P.O. and Distt. : Kokrajhar-783370(Assam)
Telephone : 03661-275513

CHARAN NARZARY

Personal

Charan Narzary was born on May 28, 1933 in a farmer's family in Hatimatha, in the Kokrajhar district of Assam. His father was Khagendranath Narzary and mother Ganeshwari Narzary. Besides working in political activities he is also a freelance Journalist.

Education

Charan Narzary completed his M.A. and LL.B. from Gauhati University.

Contribution

Charan Narzary is very active in politics. He was the founder of the Plains Tribals Council of Assam in 1967 and became its General Secretary. He represented his people as an M.L.A. for several terms. From 1977 to 1979 he served as a Member of the Lok Sabha. His essays in Bodo, Assamese and English have been published in several magazines and newspapers.

Selected Published Works

His articles are published in various magazines and newspapers of Assam.

Contact Information

Charan Narzary
8/49 Hatimatha,
P.O. : Kokrajhar,
Distt. : Kokrajhar-783370 (Assam)
Telephone : 03661-270401

JATIN KUMAR BRAHMA

Personal

Jatin Kumar Brahma was born on March 21, 1971 in Dainuguri, near Tipkai, in the district sof Kokrajhar, Assam. His father, Surendra Brahma, was very poor. Jatin therefore had a difficult childhood. Before he could complete his matriculation, the Bodo Land movement led by the All Bodo Students Union (ABSU) broke out and Jatin got involved in it heart and soul. For six years he was fully engaged, until the movement was finally suspended. He then became a teacher in ME School, Gossaingaon. Presently he is the Headmaster of the same school.

Education

Jatin received his primary schooling from his village school, but for middle and high school education he had to go a nearby village, Tipkai, where he attended Kalicharan ME School and High School.

Contribution

Brahma is a poet and short story writer. He began writing poems during high school. However, his works are yet to be published in the book form. He writes in Bodo and English.

Selected Published Works

His poems and stories are published in various Magazines and Newspapers of Assam.

Contact Information

Jatin Kumar Brahma
Village : Daimuguri, P.O. : Tipkai,
Distt : Kokrajhar,
Pin : 783337 (Assam)
Telephone : 03669-220694 (Gossaigaon)

KAMAL KUMAR BRAHMA

Personal

Kamal Kumar Brahma was born in his maternal uncle's house in the village of Dhouliguri in Kokrajhar district. His father's name was Madaram Brahma who was a Padmashri. His mother's name was Rupeshwari Brahma. He spent his childhood in his father's house at Bhavanipur in Bongaigaon. He is an eminent educationist, intellectual and orator. In 1955, while still pursuing higher education, he became a teacher in Kokrajhar High School. The same year he was married to Milapvati, the daughter of Parmeshwar Brahma of Bandoguri village situated in the district of Kokrajhar. He has seven children from his prolonged conjugal life. He is known for his immense contribution not only in literature but also in educational, social and cultural fields. As a teacher, he had a successful career, first at Kokrajhar High School and Kokrajhar College and later as the Principal of the Kokrajhar Basic Training School.

Education

Kamal Kumar Brahma got his early education at Bongaigaon. He did his graduation and post-graduation in 1958 and 1963 respectively from Guahati University.

Contribution

He began his literary career quite early in his student life. His contribution to Bodo as well as Assamese literature is considered to be valuable. Kamal Kumar Brahma is an inportant Drama writer, Poet, and Epic writer of Bodo language. In addition to this he contributed greatly to Bodo culture, especially in the development of dramas and movies. The movies **Diana** (1984) and **Jiuni Sima** (1987) are indebted, for their making, to his talent and endeavours. He, however, considers himself basically a playwright, and undoubtedly, he is a great dramatist. His main concern, in all his creative works, is the Bodo tribal culture. In his preface to the drama **Raja Iragdao**, he says, **I am at times overwhelmed with grief to think of the unfortunate gradual disintegration of Bodo (Cachari) kingdom and its ultimate destruction due to manipulation and conispracy of its enemies, induced by jealousy and ill-feelings for one another prevalent among the Bodos.** He expresses, again in the preface to his play titled **Mimasima**, his solicitude about the tendency of migration growing among the young Bodo generation.

He was from 1963 to 1975, the Secretary of Bodo Text Book Producation committe. He also served as the academic officer of the Assam Text Book Production and publication Board and made ample contribution in the fields of education, culture and language and literature. As the President of the Bodo Film Society and the Bodo Sahitya Sabha, he made great contribution to Bodo literature and culture.

He was honoured with **Bodo Sahitya Sabha Award Ransar** in 1997 for his drama **Harbadi Khomsi**.

Selected Published Works

Amarni Methai (Poetry)—2000, **Jiuni Siman** (Social drama)—1986, **Harbadi Khomsi** (Social drama)—1968, **Mandarni Modai** (Drama)—1967, **Mimani Siman** (Drama)—1964, **Unao** (Drama)—1964, **Raja Iragdau** (Historical drama)—1962, **Goronthi Gwdan Faisali** (Drama)—1957, **Goronthi** (Drama)—1954-55, **Dulali** (Assamese poems)—1954.

Contact Information

Kamal Kumar Brahma
Ward No. 7,
R.N.B. Road,
Kokrajhar, B.T.C.,
(Assam)
Pin : 783370,
Telephone : 03661-270712

KAMESWAR BRAHMA

Personal

Kameswar Brahma was born on September 1, 1940 in Bhumka village, which is under the Gossaigaon subdivision of the Kokrajhar district of Assam. His father was the late Gobinda Brahma and his mother the late Jaga Brahma. Kameshwar Brahma has been in the teaching profession since 1963, when he joined the Rupshi J.N. Academy of Dhubri district as a graduate teacher. He also taught at Dhubri Girls College as a part time lecturer until 1972. Later he joined Gossaigaon College as Head of the Department of History. In 1985 he was appointed by the Government of Assam to be D.E.E.O of Sanitpur district of Assam. Since 1985 he has also served as Principal of Gossaigaon College.

Education

Brahma received his primary education from his village LP School. For higher education he moved to Kokrajhar, where he passed the H.S.L.C. Examination at Kokrajhar Government High School. He completed pre-university and graduation in the Arts from Kokrajhar College. He finished his post-graduaion in History from Gauhati University in 1968 and obtained a Ph.D. from the same university for his research, **A Study of Socio-religious Beliefs, Practices and Ceremonies of the Bodo (with special reference to the Bodos of Kokrajhar District).**

Contribution

Brahma is an eminent Bodo short story writer and essayist. Brahma writes in Bodo, Assamese and English. He has also worked as a journalist. His published works include books on history, biography, culture and social issues. He has also written short stories for children in Bodo and also written Bodo myths and legends. **Myth of the Bodos Short Stories** (Bodo in two volumes) are under publication.

He organised many national seminars and workshops and presented papers on many topics including **Significance and Problems of Folklore Studies in North-East India and Status of Woman in Plains Tribal Societies of Assam : Tradition and Change.** He also worked for the cooperative movement.

He is the President of the Assam Sahitya Sabha, Gossaigaon Primary Committee.

He is a member of the North-East Council of Social Science Research, Shillong since 1982, and has been a Research Guide of Guahati University since 1991.

He was the recipient of **Best Citizen** of India Award, 1996, from RIFACIMENTO International, New Delhi.

Selected Published Works

A Study in Cultural Heritage of the Bodos—1999, **Raithai Bidang** (collection of essays)—1994, **Life and Works of Srimot Kalicharan Brahma**—1992, **Aspects of Social Customs of Bodos**—1989, **Boroni Harimoo** (on the cultures of Bodos, in Bodo)—1986, **Gurudev Srimot Kalicharan Brahma** (biography in Bodo)—1986, **Gossaigaon Saharar Samu Itibritta** (in Assamese)—1983, and **Bharatni Jarimin** (History of India in Bodo language)—1974.

Contact Information

Kameshwar Brahma
W/No. 4, Gossaigaon Town,
P.O. : Gossaigaon,
Distt. : Kokrajhar,
Pin : 783360 (Assam)
Telephone : 03669-220330

MADHU RAM BORO

Personal

Madhu Ram Boro was born near Hajo on November 1, 1938. He taught in schools, including the Hajo Higher Secondary School. He also worked as an Assistant Teacher at Ramdia H.E. School, Hajo Higher Secondary School, and A.K. Institute, North Guwahati. Eventually he became the Headmaster of Kachari Mahal High School, Madhukuchi (Rangia). He joined the Linguistics Department of Guahati University as a university teacher in 1975. Boro retired from service in 1998. A recipient of the Assam Government literary pension, Sri Boro is still a permanent resident of Hajo, a rural area, and spends a sizeable portion of his income on publishing his books from a printing press that is set up in a corner of his cottage. He lives a very simple life and is associated with many local social organizations.

Education

Boro passed matriculation and graduation from Guahati University, in 1955 and 1959 respectively. He obtained a Master's degree in Linguistics from Pune University in 1965. While teaching in a school in North Guwahati, he attempted the M.A. examination (in Sanskrit) at Gauhati University. However he withdrew the result because it was not to his expectation. The first postgraduate of Linguistics from the North East.

Contribution

Madhu Ram Boro is a pre-eminent writer in the Bodo language. He writes essays, poems, fictions, and grammar, particularly in Bodo. Most of his Bodo books are recognized textbooks for various levels of classes, starting from the primary to the MA level. More than twenty of his books in the Bodo language are prescribed as textbooks, including books on social studies and rapid reading. He is one of the biggest contributors to the Bodo body of literature, having written more than 70 books on different subjects involving language and literature. Boro also writes in English and Assamese. He has produced a significant amount of academic material in the Bodo language. Boro has also compiled folk tales of Bodo tribes and culture.

Boro has been felicitated with several awards : **Ideal teacher/ Literature/Artist** (Vocal Music) by Dadra/Damdama Anchalik/Hajo Sahitya Sabha, Hajo, Kamrup; **Centenary Literature/Educationist** by Hajo Anchalik Journalist's Association in 2001; Received **Felicitation in Golden Jubilee Celebration Bodo Sahitya Sabha**, Basugaon in 2002; Received **Literary Pension from Assam Government** in 2002.

He has received several awards inlcuding the **Sahitya Academy Bhasha Samman** (2002).

He is also attached to many organizations such as—**Bodo Sahitya Sabha, State Language Implementation Committee**, Administrative Terminology Committee, Assam Publication Board, Assam Textbook Production and Publication Corporation, Textbook Production, SCERT, Assam, and DPEP. He has also served as a State member in the Advisory board of the Education Dept., Assam Government.

Selected Published Works

Abouni Gami (a novel in Bodo), **Mugani Thandoi** (Full Length drama), **Mungkhlongni Hangma** (a poetry book in Bodo), **Aji Ami Kon Bate** (In Assamese), **Gomothab Solo** (In Bodo), **Guban Hadotni Solo** (Foreign tales in Bodo), **Gaholao Jaolia Dewan** (Legendary tales in Bodo).

Folk Literature

Bodo Loka Sahitya (Vol – 1)., **Bodo Loka Sahitya** (Vol – II)., **Bodo Loka Sahitya** (Vol – III)., **Bodo Sadhukatha** (In Assamese)., **Bodo Solo Batha** (In Bodo)., **Harimu aro Bodo Harimu** (In Bodo)., **Shiphung Gungang** (In Bodo).

Literature for Children: **Sisugram** (Grandmother's childhood village, in Assamese).

Life Sketch/Biography

Biplabi Bir Bishnuprasad Rabha (In Assamese), **Dr. Bhimrao Ramji Ambedkar** (In Assamese), **Maxim Gorki** (In Assamese), **Gaholao Bishnu Prasad Rabha** (In Bodo), **Dr. Bhimrao Ramji Ambedkar** (In Bodo), **Maxim Gorki** (In Bodo), **Garbonai Lamakhou Naiphinhornazo** (In Bodo).

On Language and Linguistics

In Bodo

Gejer Raokhanthi (Bodo Grammar for School level), **Godan Raokhanthi** (Bodo Grammar for H.S. Level), **Rao aro Ransai** (Grammar, essay and Treatise for H.S. College and University Level), **Godan Raokhanthi** (Grammar for College and University Level), **Jariminni Gejerjong Bodo Rao** (A History of the Bodo Language).

In Assamese

Bodo Bhasar Gathon (Bodo Language Learning Method), **Tibbat Barmi Bhasa Gosthi** (Tibeto-Burman Family of Languages).

In English

Historical Development of Bodo Language, The Bodo Structure (For M.A. Ling), **The Assamese Structure** (For M.A. Ling), **Assamese and Bodo: A Comparative and Constructive Study** (A Textbook of English Second Paper for High and H. S. School)—1987.

Criticism

In English

The History of Bodo Literature (For M.A. Bodo), **Gariminni Nojorao** (composed and edited).

In Bodo

Thunlai aro Bodo Thunlai (Literature and Bodo Literature), **Bodo Thunlaini Saorijthayari Jarimin** (Critical History of Bodo Literature), **Bodo Raithaini Lu** (Criticism of Bodo Prose Literature), **Bodo Khanthaini Lu** (Criticism of Bodo Poetical Literature).

Edited Books

Garimini Gaherjong Bodo Thunlai (A History of Bodo Literature), **Bodo English-Hindi Dictionary** (B.S.S. C.I.I.L. Mysore), **Multilingual Dictionary including Bodo** (Natun Sahitya Parishad), **Multilingual Dictionary including Bodo** (C.I.I.I. Mysore).

Other notable books

History of Bodo Literature (in English), **Historical Development of Bodo Language, Bodo Loko Sahitya, Harimu aro Bodo Harimu, Thunlai aro Bodo Thunlai, Bodo Thunlaini Saoraithaiary Jarimin,** and **Rao aro Ransai.**

Books in print : Bodo–English Dictionary (Guwahati: N.L. Publications).

Worked as a Journalist and Editor of : Sambad Saptahik (Multilingual news weekly including Assamese, English, Boro and other tribal languages of N.E. India), **Aromar Janajati** (Multilingual magazine published in leading tribal languages including Bodo of N.E. India in Assam at present Editor, **Asomiya Ganamat** (Newspaper).

Contact Information

Madhu Ram Boro
Village & Post : Hajo
District : Kamrup (Assam)
C/o Hareswar Das, Editor,
Asomiya Ganamat, Lachit Nagar, Guwahati-7
Telephone : 0361-2460435 Fax : 0361-2460437
Website : www.ganamat.com
E-mail : ganamat2003@yahoo.co.in

MADA RAM BRAHMA

Personal

Mada Ram Brahma was born at Gunikhusa in the District of undeuided Goalpara District in Assam and died on September 6, 1990 at Runath Brahma Civil Hospital, Kokrajhar.

Contribution

Late Mada Ram Brhama who was an educationist and linguist, a noted Bodo writer and social worker was awarded the **PADMASHRI** by R. Vengkataraman, the honourable President of India for his contribution in the fields of Bodo Culture, Society, language and literature with his valuable contributions.

Boroni Gudi Sibsa Arw Aroj or Principal Concept of the Boros, Faith and Hymms' (1996) was the first Boro book written by **Padmashri Mada Ram Brahma**. This book contains prayer songs sung during **Kherai** festival to appease **Bathou** the main God of the Boros.

Mada Ram Brahma being assisted by Runath Brahma compiled a book by the name of **Khanthai Methai** which means Peoms and songs.

Mada Ram Brahma's **Raimali** is a social drama depicting the picture of ideal Boro girl **Raimali** engaged in social, religious and cultural activities. While his another drama **Dimapur Raijw Bainai** meaning the fall of **Dimapur Kingdom** has pathos indescription and tragic in fact.

Sadang Bairagi is his another social drama whrere the character of simplicity and sacrifice for others has been depicted through the activitier of Sadang the medicant.

The short book written by Madaram Brahma was **Phangseao Bibar Barnwi** meaning **two flowers in the branch** which depicts the idea on deep rooted love of two souls. The book has two other short stories being edited in one, having social pictures.

Published Work

Boroni Gudi Sibsa Arw Aroj—1926, Khanthai Methai, Raimali, Dimapur Raijw Bainai, Phangseao Bibar Barnwi two flowers in the branch.

MAHADEV UZIR BASUMATARY

Personal

Mahadev Uzir Basumatary was born in a Boro family on June 21, 1974, to Gopal Ch. Basumatary and Jayanti Basumatary. Since 2000 he is serving as Technical Adviser (Agricultural Expert) for DUBAA, a non-political organisation that works for the Boro farming community. Mahadev Uzir Basumatary is a senior research fellow in the Department of Agronomy, Assam Agriculture University, Jorhat.

Education

He is a post-graduate in Agriculture from Assam Agricultural University. Mahadev Uzir Basumatary passed all his academic examinations in the first division.

Contribution

Basumatary writes articles and essays, mostly on Agricultural topics. A number of his articles and essays have been published in leading Bodo and English magazines of Assam.

Some of his important articles are: **Traditional cultivation practices of the Boros**, published in Souvenir on the occasion of the National Boro Mela (New Delhi—2003); **Growth, yield attributes and yield of summer green gram as affected by levels of Phosphorus and lime**, published in Journal of the Agricultural Science Society of North-East India in December—2001.

Contact Information

Mahadev Uzir Basumatary
C/o Shri Gopal Ch. Basumatary
Depot Road, W/.No-4
P.O. and Dist : Kokrajhar, Pin : 783370 (Assam)
Telephone : 03661-271240

MANGAL SINGH HAZOWARI

Personal

Dr. Mangal Singh Hazowari was born to the late Khasia Hazowari and Khuji Hazowari on March 1, 1954. He has been a teacher since 1978, working as a lecturer in different colleges in Kokrajhar. He presently serves as Principal of Government C.T.E., Kokrajhar. He has awarded from the International Business Council, New Delhi.

Education

Mangal Singh Hazowari is an M.A. and Ph.D. from Gauhati University on **The Traditional Bodo Festival: A Critical Study.**

Contribution

Dr. Mangal Singh Hazowari is an eminent writer in Bodo and Assamese. He writes poems, essays, short stories, dramas and biographies in Bodo, Assamese, Bengali and English. Dr. Hazowari's contribution to literature is considerable in various genres and he has several published works to his credit. A number of his books have been prescribed in the school, college and university curriculum of Bodo language and literature.

He has also been actively associated in different capacities with the Bodo Sahitya Sabha, of which he is a life member.

He has received several awards from institutions including the All India Achievers Conference, New Delhi.

Selected Published Works

Harimu Arw Swdwmsri, Jothai Bidang, Raithai Bihung, Raithai Arw Sansri (collection of essays)—2002, **Thwijwng Lirnay Dwngse Khonthai** (collection of poems)—2002, **Bathou Aroj** (prayer songs), **Jiuni Khonthai Methai, Fwisali Andwni Solo** (collection of short stories), **Swmdwm** (full length drama), **Jaolia Dewan** (full length drama), **Jwhwlao Dwimalu** (full length drama),

Siman (collection of one-act plays), **Padmashri Modaram Brahma** (biography).

Contact Information

Dr. Mangal Singh Hazowari
Kokrajhar, Ward No.-7
PO and Dist : Kokrajhar, Pin : 733370 (Assam)
Telephone : 03661-270029 (R) 270683 (O)

MANORANJAN LAHARY

Personal

Manoranjan Lahary is a versatile Bodo writer of short stories, poetry, essays, novels, dramas and one-act plays. He was born on February 2, 1936. His father's name was Basant Kumar Lahary. He chose teaching as his career and even now is associated as a guest lecturer with the Guahati University at its Kokrajhar campus. He entered this profession in 1963 when he joined Kokrajhar College as a lecturer in English. He became Principal, B.Ed. College, Kokrajhar in 1981 and subsequently moved to another B.Ed. College at Dhubri as its Principal. He is now settled with his family in Kokrajhar, Assam.

Education

Lahary passed his matriculation examination from Ableyasari High School, Abhayapuri in 1953. He graduated in 1957 from the famous Cotton College of Guwahati. He finished his M.A. in 1963 from Gauhati University. Subsequently, in 1972, he obtained a B.T. degree.

Contribution

Manoranjan Lahary made contribution to almost all the genres of the literature, viz. fiction, poetry, prose and drama. He also edited several magazines, journals and souvenirs, viz. **Okhaphor** (1954-55), **Asorman Janajati** (1975, 1976 and 1977), **Souvenir, Bodo Sahitya Sabha** (1966), **Souvenir, Bodo Sahitya Sabha Silver Jubilee Celebration** (1977), **Souvenir, All Assam Sangeet Silpi Somaroh** (Annual Session-1984).

He is associated with various literary associations and organizations in different capacities, such as, Member, Expert Committee for Boro Language Implementation (Government of Assam) (1963), Member, Boro Text Books Production Committee (1962), Chairman, Sub-Committee for History of Bodo Literature,

Founder President, Boro Writers' Academy(1984), Member, Goodwill Mission to N.C. Hills (1985), Member, Boro Writers' Goodwill Mission to Affected Areas (1989), Chairman, Boro Syllabus Sub-Committee (1992), etc.

He is the recipient of several awards, viz., Literary Award by State Government (1994), Kokrajhar District Boro Sahitya Sabha Award, 1994, Award by Kokrajhar Anchalik Bodo Sahitya, Boro Writers' Academy Award, Gandhi Hindustani Sahitya Sabha Award, 1999, Someswari Award, Boro Sahitya Sabha (2003), Bishnu Rava Award, Assam State Government (2004), PG Boro Students' Association Award (2004), etc.

Selected Published Works

Poetry Collections

Ang Phoiphingori, 1995, **Maflafa Aru Gufun Gufan Khonthai,** 1993, **Maflafa,** 1979, **My verses** (English), **Singing down the Rani** (English).

Prose Works

Gwdan Boro (Collection of critical essays), **Navjr** (Collection of critical essays), **In the Realm of Thought** (Critical essays in English), **A Study of Boro Folk Songs** (Research work in English).

Short Story Collections

Crolo Bidang, Bojoi, Gaodany.

Novels

Kharlung, Hainamuli, Rebecca, Alaishri, Dainee, Subungsa.

Drama

Anari, Hangma Hangsa, Maoriasaran.

One-act Plays

Mohorsirini Simang, Orangri Bibar, Barsa Bibar Chirinai, Rangkhini, Balhangkhani Unao, Gauba Gao Lama, Bima, Hinjao Naino Thangnaiyar, Dengkho.

Life Sketches

Satish Ch. Banty, Rup Nath Brahma, Padmashri MR Brahmo, P.C. Brahma.

Contact Infromation

Manoranjan Lahary
R.N.B. Road,
PO : Kokrajhar & Distt : Kokrajhar, (Assam)
Telephone : 03661-270822

MUKUT PRASAD BORO

Personal

Shri Mukut Prasad Boro was born on December 1, 1969. His father was the late Deben Boro and his mother Smt. Sumati Bala Boro. He actively participates in many social, cultural and educational activities. He has been in the teaching profession for several years. Presently, he is working as an L.D. Assistant at K.B. Deulkuchi H.S.D. School. He lives in Kachari Solmari village (Rangia) in the Kamrup District of Assam with his wife, Dulumani Basumatary, and his two daughters, Swrangmani Lahari and Dodere Mainao Lahari.

Education

Boro received his primary education from Chirakhundi L.P. School. In 1986 he passed the H.S.L.C. Examination from K.B. Deulkuchi High School and passed the Higher Secondary Examination in 1992 from K.B. Denlkuchi Higher Secondory School. He later received admittance to L.C. Bhorali College, Guwahati, but was unable to complete his studies due to family obligations.

Contribution

Mukut Prasad Boro is a young Bodo short story writer, essayist and critic. Mukut Prasad Boro has also published three collections of Bodo short stories.

Boro's articles, criticism and essays have been published in various magazines and newspapers. Boro has also edited several magazines and souvenirs and worked briefly in journalism. Presently, he is a correspondent with **Bodosa,** a weekly Bodo newspaper published in Kokrajhar, Assam. He has also been the chief editor of **Rwinakhunagri** (Issue numbers 6, 7 and 8 of 2001, 2002 and 2003), an annual journal of the Bodo Sahitya Sabha, Rangiya as well as of **Smiritigrantha** (1997, Tri-Lingual) A Souvenir of K.B. Denlkuchi H.S. School.

Selected Published Works

Garbwnai Sanfwrkhow Nagirnanai—2003, Bwdwr Baoli Gwsw—2002, Gwrwnthia Swrni—1995.

Contact Information

Mukut Prasad Boro
Kachari Solmari,
P.O. : Kachari Solmari,
Distt : Kamrup, Pin : 781354 (Assam)
Telephone : 03621-242603

PHUKAN CHANDRA BASUMATARY

Personal

Phukan Chandra Basumatary was born on December 1, 1967 in the Bagona Bennabari village, P.O. Bongaon, District-Barpeta in Assam. He is the youngest son of Goneswar Basumatary and Smt. Alaishri Basumatary. He is presently a lecturer in the Bodo Language at Rangia College in Rangia, Assam.

Education

Basumatary is an M.A. and M.Phil. He did his M.Phil. in Folklore Research. He is currently in the process of completing his Ph.D. on the topic, **A Study on Cultural and Linguistic Affinities of the Bodos and Rabhas of Assam.**

Contribution

Phukan Chandra Basumatary is a young poet, critic and essay writer. He has written five books in Boro Language, one poetry book, two criticism and one book is Translation into Boro. One book in Boro language also is writen by him. Basumatary has four articles in English, fifteen in Assamese, thirty in Bodo, and one in Bengali (translated from original Assamese) as well as a few research papers on language and linguistics which have also been published in different magazines and research Journals. Basumatary has also participated in different state and national level seminars and workshops on topics like **Current Trends in the Literature of North-East and Problems** and **Possiblities of Little Magazines of the North-East.** The Central Institute of Indian Languages, Mysore and National Book Trust, New Delhi have also invited him as a resource person.

He is a member of the Bhasha Samman jury for Bodo Language and Literature sponsored by Sahitya Akademi. He is also a member of the syllabus committee of Guahati University for P.G. level (Bodo) since 2001.

Selected Published Works

Nwibe Lamazwng Nwng Phwiywmwnbwla (poetry book)—2003, **Criticism on Twentieth Century Boro Poetry** (in Boro)—2002, **Robinson Crusoe** (Translated abridged version in Boro)—2002, **Boro Language and Literature** (in Boro)—2000, **Morphology of Boro Language** (in Boro)—2000.

Contact Information

Phukan Chandra Basumatary
Rangia College Rangia,
Dist. : Kamrup (Assam)

PRABAN BARGOYARI

Personal

Praban Bargoyari is an eminent Bodo writer. He was born on May 10, 1960. He also writes in Assamese and English. He is a born leader and signs of this quality were visible in him right from his childhood. He was Vice-President and General Secretary of Kokrajhar College Bodo Students' Literary Forum of Guahati University. Blessed with eloquence of excellence, he was one of the best debator and from 1987 to 1990 served in All India Radio, Guwahati as an announcer. He is working in Sales Tax Office, Department of Taxation, Government. of Assam and is a member of the Oron, Forest Conservation Trust Board.

Education

He is M.A. in History from Gauhati University and achieved first class second position in the university.

Contribution

Though he has published only one book titled the **Observation and the Views**, his articles and essays have appeared in several leading newspapers, periodicals and journals. He also contributed in compilation of **Anglo-Bodo Dictionary**. Besides writing, he has edited many literary magazines, the most remarkable among them is the **Orkhi**, which is considered to be one of the most revolutionary and radical Bodo news fortnightly. Quite a few journals and magazines such as **Gangga, Sushraoti, Alaikunggri**, etc., published in connection with seminars of national level have also been edited by him.

In 2003 he participated in National lavel Seminar organised by Gandhi Hidustani Sahitya Sabha Delhi and threw light on the inportance of Tribal languages by reading a paper—**21st century : Future of Tribal Languages & their Role in National Integration.**

Presently, he is the chief editor of the **Bodo** the mouthpiece of Bodo Sahitya Sabha.

He is also associted with Sobha Brahma Trust Board, Bodo cultural Musicum Foundation Trust and National Institute of Bodology, Kokrajhar.

Selected Published Works

Observation and the views

Contact Information

Praban Bargoyari
Boltola, Madan Gaon,
Guwahati-28 (Assam)
Phone : 0361-2227856

PREMA NONDO MACHAHARY

Personal

Prema Nondo Machahary was born on January 28, 1958 in village Dhaigaon in the Goalpara District of Assam. While still an infant, he moved to the Karbi Anglong district with his father, Chandi Charan Machahary and mother, Parmeshwari Machahary. Machahary is presently a lecturer in Political Science at Thong Nokbe College of Karbi Anglong.

Machahary began his career as a manager in a cooperative society. Subsequently, he founded Langhin Girls' High School, where he also worked as headmaster. He changed his profession again and joined the Langpi Dehangi Rural Bank as Branch Manager. Dissatisfied, he resigned from this job too, and finally settled on a career in education. Machahary is married and has two daughters and a son.

Education

Machahary passed the H.S.L.C. examination in 1974, from Langhin Pamgaon High School. He completed his graduation in Arts in 1980 from Diphu Government College. In 1982 he did his postgraduation in Political Science from Guahati University. In February 2003 he received a Ph.D. from Gauhati University for his research on the subject **The Socio-Political Life of the Boros in Karbi Anglong district of Assam.**

Contribution

Machahary writes in Bodo, Assamese and English. His reputation rests on his poems, stories, dramas and essays, which have appeared regularly in various magazines, newspapers and seminars. Four Bodo video dramas were produced under his direction. They are **Gwrbwni Mijing** (A dream of the heart), **Khithirni** (A fire of revenge), **Hangmat** (A high hope) and **Nwngni Thakai Angni Jwnwm** (My birth is for you). These dramas received wide appreciation from the public. He also acted in two of these dramas and composed most of the songs and lyrics for three of them.

Selected Published Works

Samajik Aru Rajnotik Potobhumit Karbi Anglongar Boro-Kochari-Sokol (in Assamese)—1999, **Kopili Upatyakat Borosokolor Otit Aru Borotaman Samajik Jivanar Somi Itibritta** (A socio-historical book in Assamese)—1999, **Onthay Gufur Hajoni Solo** (A storybook in Bodo)—1997, **Dominated Tribals of Assam**—1997, **Ethno-Political Identity Crises Among the Tribals of North-East India**—1996, **Burlong Buthur Hayenao Bodoni Sodomsri** (In Bodo)—1996, **Nonguboi Subung Dhorom are Mugani Sabsin Joholao** (A religious book in Bodo)—1994.

Contact Information

Prema Nondo Machahary
Village : Pandugaon,
P.O. : Langhin Tiniali-782441
Dist. : Karbi Anglong
(Assam)
Telephone : 03674-296687 (R)/299866 (O)

PURNA BORO

Personal

Purna Boro was born on October 14, 1949 and brought up at Chila Katamur village in Kamrup district. His father's name is Mani Ram Boro and mother's name is Reba Boro.

He taught for two years in Chagsari Girls High School and then in 1974 joined Goreswar College as a lecturer. He developed an interest in politics after the Emergency in 1977.

He was elected to the Assam Legislative Assembly in two consecutive elections of 1978 and 1983 as a CPI (M) candidate. Presently he is a state committee member of CPI (M) and is the President of the Assam State's Kisan Sabha.

Education

He passed H.S.L.C. Examination from Changsari High School. He studied B.A. Honours in Assamese in Cotton College, and did his M.A. from Gauhati University.

Contribution

His contribution as a writer is in the form of articles and essays. He mostly writes on socio-economic, political, and current issues. Many of his articles have been published in magazines and journals like **Ganshakti, Danik Assam** and **Danik Janabhumi,** a widely distributed daily newspaper of Assam. Besides being a writer of socio-cultural issues, he is also interested in music and singing songs for AIR in Guva Bani. He visited Utkal University, Bhuwneshwar (Orissa) as a member of a cultural troupe from Gauhati University and also performed cultural programmes.

Contact Information

Purna Boro
LIG-5, Flat-1, House Complex, Hengrabari
P.O. : Assam Sachivalaya
Dishpur, Guwahati-6
Distt.: Kamrup (Assam)
Telephone : 0361-2225799

RAMDAS BORO

Personal

Ramdas Boro was born in Chutiapara village in Nalbari District, Assam, on October 11, 1936. His father was Batimal Boro and his mother was Dandi Boro.

Boro established Athiabari Vidyamandir High School in 1961 and became the principal of this school. He also worked as the founder since its upgradation to a higher secondary school in 1979 to 1983. He was the principal of Mushalpur College from 1991 to 1993. Boro was also officiating principal of Thomana College from 1994 to 1997. He was also the head examiner of the Secondary Education Board in Assam.

Boro has been very active in politics, contesting Legislative Assembly elections in 1983, 1985, 1991 and 1996. He also served as a public servant and as Chief Administrator of the Nalbari Mahakuma Parishad from 1983 to 1985. He is the President of his local panchayat and also President of the Block Education Committee of the Sarva Shiksha Abhiyan Mission. In 1972 he founded the **Dularai Asom Bodo Bathousali** (Bathou temple).

Education

Boro matriculated in the first division with distinction in Mathematics and Sanskrit from Patacharkuchi Vidyapith in 1955. He passed Intermediate of Arts in the first division from Cotton College in 1957. In 1959 he did his Bachelor of Arts from Cotton College, Guwahati. Boro did his Master of Arts in History in 1964 and ET in Education did in 1979 from Gauhati University.

Contribution

Boro writes in Assamese, English and Bodo. Over one hundred of his articles are published in different magazines and souvenirs. He produced an Assamese translation of Rabindranath Tagore's

Gitanjalee. He also wrote **Godan Bithrahu**—classes I & II. These two books are integrated as text-*cum*-workbooks for classes I & II, developed by SCERT, Assam in collaboration with DPEP, Assam through workshops. This has been adopted into Bodo from the original Assamese and approved by the government of Assam and published by the Assam State Textbook Production and Publication Corporation Limited, Guwahati. He has also been a contributor to All India Radio.

Ramdas Boro was awarded the **Someswari Brahma Thunlai Bantha** (Literary Award) by the Bodo Sahitya Sabha in 1997.

Boro has served as the President of the Nalbari District Bodo Sahitya Sabha and Vice President of the All Bodo Sahitya Sabha. He was selected for a state literary life pension by the Assam Government in 1995.

Selected Published Works

Daukha Dandi (Folktale)—2003, **Guwahati Bishnu Rabha Dhabo Urulangkhwe** (Bodo poetry)—2000/1974, **Debajanee Aru Kach** (Assamese playlet in verse)—2000, **Jeevan Dyoti** (Assamese mother tongue like Rubaiyat)—2000, **Fwifin** (Bodo poetry)—1976, **Bithorai** (Bodo primer)—1974, **Vyabadhan** (Assamese social novel)—1964, **Sangrema** (short story) and **Alari** (translated works)—1958.

Contact Information

Ramdas Boro
Village : Chutiapara
Athiabari, Nalbari, Pin : 781377 (Assam)

RATAN KUMAR RAY HAJONG

Personal

Ratan Kumar Ray Hajong was born in 1958 in a little-known village of the Mymensingh District in East Pakistan. 'Bhuyan Para', as his village was known, was a land blessed with rich harvests, beautiful natural beauty and folk music as well as a rich folk culture, which formed the very essence of its being.

Unfortunately, political and communal factors forced him to leave this veritable paradise. For a while his family lived in a refugee camp in the Goalpara District of Assam. Then, between 1963 and 1964, they were rehabilitated in the area. It was there that he first came into contact with and was totally enraptured by the Bodo culture and he started training in Bodo music and dance. He considers his marriage to Pronoti in 1985 to be a great event in his life.

Education

Ray was unable to complete schooling beyond the primary level because of poverty and the associated problems of inadequate food, clothing and shelter, which forced him to work as cowherd in a neighbouring Bodo village. His life was very difficult and in spite of poverty and other adverse conditions he managed to receive a High School Certificate. His career then followed an upward path, starting from cowherding, then running a *Pan* shop, working as a Chawkidar to becoming an Akashvani and Doordarshan artist and producer of number of documentaries. He ultimately became a layout artist in a newspaper.

Contribution

Ray has exhibited his paintings in several solo exhibitions and numerous other exhibitions all over India. Now he is an established artist. He has three publications to his credit. In addition to writing, Ray participates in several cultural activities in his area. He is the founder of **Monbikash**, an organization that seeks to promote adolescent talent in the North-East region. He also publishes and edits a magazine for children by the name **Monbikash.**

Selected Published Works

Hajong Samaj Aru Sanskritit Dristapat (relevent data information on the Hajang)—2003, **Tendrala Phul** (self-composed Hajong, modern song) —1997, **Dohsamayar Mukhamukhi** (self-composed Assamese poems)—1994.

Contact Information

Ratan Kumar Ray Hajong
The Assam Tribune, Tribune building, Chandmari
Guwahati–781003 (Assam)
Telephone: 0361-2660739 (R) / 2661360 (O)

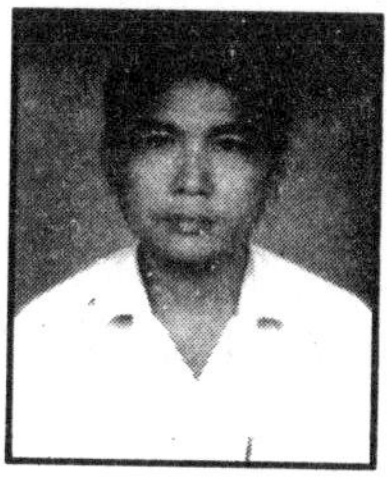

ROMA KANTA BASUMATARY

Personal

Roma Kanta Basumatary was born to Jagya Ram Basumatary and Guneshwari Basumatary on January 1, 1967 in Khandikar, a village in the Kamrup District of Assam. He is a teacher by profession.

Education

Basumatary has completed his education up to the high school level.

Contribution

Roma Kanta Basumatary is a poet, essayist and short story writer. He writes in Bodo. Basumatary has published three poetry collections, a short story collection and a biography. A number of his articles have also appeared in Assamese. Basumatary is the editor of **Laithun**, a journal of the Bodo Writers' Academy, and is the chief editor of **Nerson**, a Bodo quarterly magazine. He has also served as editor of **Rainakhungri**, the mouth-piece of the Rangia District Bodo Sahitya Sabha (1994-1996) and **Rounia**, the mouth-piece of the Rangia Anchalik Bodo Sahitya Sabha (1993-2005). His 25 poems translated from Bodo to Assamese and several articles written in Bodo have also been published. He also participated in dance programmes Doordarshan as well as in poetry recitation and talk programmes on All India Radio.

Roma Kanta Basumatary is an active member of the Bodo Sahitya Sabha. He is also the editor for the Bodo Writers' Academy.

Selected Published Works

Life and Creation (biography in Bodo)—2002, **Right** (poetry in Bodo),—2001, **Who is Guilty** (short story in Bodo)—1995, **To Revolutionary Friend** (poetry in Bodo)—1993, **War Poem** (poetry in Bodo)—1993.

Contact Information

Roma Kanta Basumatary
Khandikar, P.O. : Deulkuchi,
Distt. : Kamrup (Assam), Pin- 781354.

RUPNATH BRAHMA

Personal

Rupnath Brahma was born at a village called 'Owabari' in a well to do family on June 15, 1902. His father's name was Dhwajendra Brahma and his mother's name was Khwadwmshri. As a student, Rupnath Brahma was closely associated with various student organisations. He was very enthusiastic about the various needs and problems of the students Organisations. He organised Boro Student's Association in 1918. Rupnath Brahma served as the genral secretay of the Goalpara Boro Chatra Sonmiloni (Goalpara Bodo Student's Association) from 1918 to 1928 consecutively.

After obtaining law degree in 1928, Rupnath Brahma started his legal practice in the lower court, Dhubri. He continued his profession till he was elected. Member of Assam Legislative Assembly in 1937 in British peried. He became a member of Local Board, Dhubri. He did many developmnet works for the upliftment of the rural people. His contributions towards the development of the rural mass irrespective of cast and creedis.

He served as Minister of Assam holding diffrent portfolios from 1938 to 1967 with reputation as a sincere, honest and dedicated Minister. In the middle of 1967 he was elected a member of Parliament but unfurtunately he could attend only one session of Parliament before his death. He established a record of being inducted as a Minister for a long period of 29 years from 1938 to 1967 consecutively. At his initiative the Kokrajhar sub-Division was created in 1957.

Rupnath Brahma died on the 23rd January, 1968 at 3.30 A.M. He breathed his last at the Kokrajhar Civil Hospital whose foudation stone he had laid himself.

Education

His father took keen interest for the education of Rupnath. He was admitted to the Kokrajhar Higher Primary School. He passed the Matriculation Examination in 1921 in 1st Division. He took his B.A.

degree in Arts from Cotton College, Guwahati in 1925. He studied both M.A. and Law simultaneously at Calcutta University College and passed Law examination in 1928.

Contribution

Rupnath Brahma was a good essayist and poet. He published his Bodo poems in an anthology called Khantai Methai in collaboration with Padmashri Late Mada Ram Brahma. Most of his poems were dialactic and meta-physical in nature with romantic underone to some extent. His poetry highlights his philosophy of life. With his common place subject matters, he could express the lofty ideals. He wrote a book entitled **Boro Jatir Parichay** which was highly appreciated by the readers. He was a regular contributors of articles to journals published from the Assam Sahitya Sabha and the Assam Sangeet Natak Accademy of which he was one of the sponsors.

He was associated with the publications of some of the Bodo Souvenirs and Journals, particularly the Bibar, edited by late Satish Chandra Basumatary. He contributed Bodo poems and essays to the Bibar, the first Bodo Jounral that heralded the new era in Bodo literaure.

Rupnath Brahma was keenly intersted in the matter of revival and development of folk songs and folk dances of the indigenous people of Assam in general and of the Tribal people of Assam in particular. Through his help a Bodo Cultural Troupe got the chance for the first time to participate in the Republic day in New Delhi in 1956. He encouraged people to form cultural organisation.

He was one of the pioneers for the formation of Sangeet Natak Academy.

Contact Information

Rupnath Brahma
Ward No.-7, R.N.B. Road, Kokrajhar
B.T.C. (Assam) Pin-783370

SOBHA BRAHMA

Personal

Sobha Brahma was born on October 14, 1929 in Gossaigaon, Assam. He is a member of the Bodo-Kachari Tribe. Brahma worked as an art teacher at Tarini Chowdhury HSMP School, Guwahati, from 1957 to 1958. He participated in the decoration of the All India Congress session held at Pragjyotishpur in 1958. In 1959 Brahma was awarded a research scholarship by the Department of Tribal Culture and Folklore, Gauhati University. He subsequently made a tour of the tribal areas of the Bodos, Rabhas and Dimasa Kacharis for the study of their artistic materials, including their rich collection of variegated fabric designs. From 1960 onwards Brahma worked as a teacher at the School of Art and Crafts, Assam, which later became a college with a Bachelor of Fine Arts degree course under his stewardship. He was principal of the College from 1964 to 1989.

Education

Brahma attended Cotton College, Guwahati, from 1948 to 1952. He received his artistic education at Kala Bhawan Santiniketan from 1952 to 1957, under Silpacharya Nandala Bose, Dhirendra Krishana Dev Barman, Ramkinkar Baij, and others. In 1956 he participated at the 4th International Art Students Exhibition held in Prague, Czechoslovakia.

Contribution

Brahma is a renowned author, sculptor and painter in the North-Eastern States. He writes in Bodo, Assamese, English and Bengali. Besides being a writer of essays, biographies and memoirs, he is also a film director. Brahma has also translated importants art book into Assames. His paintings have been featured in numerous solo exhibitions throughout India. His art has also been shown in Dacca, Bangladesh; Sofia, Bulgaria; Rome, Italy; and Prague, Czech Republic.

His work is part of collections at the Government Museum, Chadigarh, the Assam State Museum, Lalit Kala Akademi and several government departments in Assam, as well as private collections in Assam, Shillong, Bombay and West Germany.

He has received felicitations from several social, cultural and art educational organizations such as the Assam Sahitya Sabha, the Bodo Sahitya Sabha, Kollol Gosthi of Nagaon, the Artists Guild of Guwahati, the State Bank of India and the Deputy Commissioner's Employees Association of Guwahati. In February 2000 he was Artist-in-residence at the Regional Lalit Kala Kendra, Kolkata.

Brahma is a former member of the Central Lalit Kala Akademi, New Delhi and the Assam Textbook Production Corporation.

Brahma currently serves as Vice Chairman of the Anundoram Borooah Institute of Language, Art and Culture, Guwahati.

Brahma received the **Assam Shilpi Dibash Award** in 1977, the Assam Government **Artists Pension** in 1990, the **Kamal Kumari Borooah Foundation Award for Culture** (National) in 1999, and the **Assam State Bishnu Rabha Award** in 1996.

Selected Published Works

Bhartiya Chitra-Kala (translation in Assamese), **Gwdan Uji** (Bodo), **Silpakala Navajanma** (Assamese).

Contact Information

Sobha Brahma
House No. 215, Dhirenpara,
PO. : Dhiranpara,
Dist. : Kamrup-781025 Assam
Telephone : 2471295

SWARNA PRABHA CHAINARY

Personal

Swarna Prabha Chainary was Born on December 30, 1971 in the village of Napara, P.O. Howly, Dist. Barpeta, Assam. She is the eldest daughter of Shri Girish Chandra Chainary and Smt. Jayanti Chainary. She presently works as a lecturer in the Department of Modern Indian Languages (Bodo), Gauhati University.

Education

Chainary in an M.A. and LL.B. from Gauhati University and Government Law College respectively. She is currently engaged in research entitled **Bodo and Garo : A Comparative Linguistic Analysis** for the completion of her Ph.D.

Contribution

Swarna Prabha Chainary is a versatile young writer of short stories, essays and criticism. She also translates Assamese and English works into Bodo. Chainary writes in Bodo, Assamese and English. Her literary contribution includes a book of criticism on Bodo drama, entitled **Boro Phaothaini Bizirany** and five translated books from English and Assamese into Bodo. Chainary has also published research articles in three different journals in Assam. She is a member of the Linguistic Society of India, Pune and the Assam Research Society, Assam. She has participated in several national-level seminars and workshops and presented papers on various topics including a comparative study of Bodo and Garo literature.

Selected Published Works

Bodo Phaothaini Bizirnay (criticism on Bodo drama)—2002, **Benjamin Franklin** (translated from Assamese)—2002, **Etoa Mundaya Daohayao Derhabay** (Etoa Munda Won the Battle) translated from English, **Dwngse Khwiphwdni Solo** (A tale of trouble), **translated from English, and Khebse Gongse Gamiyao** (Once in a village). All are published by National Book Trust, New Delhi. She also has a translation by the name of **Zwngni Buhum** (from Assamese).

Contact Address

Swarna Prabha Chainary
Department of MIL
Gauhaty University
GNB Nagar, Guwahaty-14
Telephone : 03621-241436 (R)

MANORANJAN MARAK

Personal

Manoranjan Marak was born on April 1, 1946 in Ballamguri (Oxiguri), under the Bijni Sub-Division in Bongalgaon District. He is from the Garo Community and belongs to the Scheduled Tribe (P) of Assam. His father was Medhar Sangma and his mother Jamini Marak. Marak's mother and father died during his childhood, and he eventually had to leave his native village and live with relatives in North Salmara. His wife Renuka Sangama died in 1998. He was a football player at the district level and won many shields. Marak currently works as a teacher. He was appointed assistant teacher in the Garo Baptist Union Government provincialised ME School in 1967, and was promoted to Headmaster in 1990. He retired in 2004.

Education

Marak began his high school education in North Salmara. He passed the matriculation examination under Gauhati University in 1961 from North Salmara Durgaprasad Memorial High School and graduated from Abhayapuri College, Gauhati University in 1975. He had to live in a miserable condition because of poverty while completing his education.

Contribution

Marak is a Garo writer. Instead of writing in English or Garo, Marak writes in Assamese because he feels that due to the language constraint most of the aspects of traditional Garo culture remain unknown to the non-Garo people, except those very few who are highly educated. For this reason he became a freelance journalist and joined the **Dainik Asomia**, a daily newspaper of Assam, as an honorary reporter. His articles on the Garo community have been published widely by Assamese newpapers like **The Assam Bani, The Agradut, The Notun Din** and **the Asomiya Khobor**. He has also been published in the English-language magazine **Honesty**, which is edited by Gojanan Roy. He was chief editor of the Garo magazine **Balgawa** (Blossom) in 1990. Three of Marak's books have been published and two books are currently under publication.

He, later, participated in the workshop organised by Central Institute of Indian Language, Mysore in 2nd to 6th June, 1992 in NE Hills University Shillong and submitted a paper on Garo kinship terms. He also, participated in seminars organised by the Central Institution, Mysore held in Manipur University, Dibrugarh University and Guahati University respectively and submitted his research papers on the Garo Language.

Selected Published Works

Khagarpur Maha-Rani Pujar Chomu Bibaran—2000, **Garo Bhasa Sikhsar Patoni**—1989, **Garo Sokolar Jatia Utsob Wangala**—1986-87. **Garo Somajor Riti-Niti–Part-I** is under publication.

His article published in Magzines include

Root of the Garo's folk belief—1992, **Marriage System of the Garo Society**—1987, July 1st in **Argadut** Newspaper, **The Garos of Assam and their problem**—Published in **Ajir Batori**, **Creation of widow marriage in ancient Garo Society**—**Dipak** in 1965, Edited by the Late Atul Hazarika, a famous writer of Assam, **Activities of the Garo women in the life of Garo Society**—Published in Souvenir **Golpityika**. All Assam Women Writers Association held at Goalpara in 2000.

Contact Information

Manoranjan Marak
At Village : Khagarpur,
P.O. : Khagarpur,
Pin-783383
Distt. : Bongaigaon,
(Assam)

BIDOR SING KRO

Personal

Bidor Sing Kro was born in Assam on June 27, 1957. His home is in Rongtheang Diphu, a village in the Karbi Anglong district. He belongs to the Karbi tribe.

Education

Kro is a graduate.

Contribution

Bidor Sing Kro writes prose and poetry in both Karbi and Assamese. Kro is a prolific writer. Two of his most noteworthy books are in the Karbi language. Most of his writing focuses on Karbi society. He uses both Roman and Assamese scripts to write poetry, essays, novels and short stories.

In 1978 he received an award for his poetry from the **Karbi Lammet Amei**. In 2001 he received the **Longchor Award**, given by Longchor Publications.

Kro is curently President of **Karbi Lammet Amei**. A poetry collection, novel, short story collection and essay collection are currently being published. His poems and articles have also been published in **Saptarkhi Magazine.**

Selected Published Works

Akemi Karbi Lamthe Amarjong (a Karbi dictionary)––2002, **Rup Taineh**—1998. by Karbi Lammiet, Amei, **Diphu Ser Longchor** (A collection of essays on the Karbi cultures, traditions). **Larta** (A collection of folk songs of the Karbis)

Edited Books

Pengsomir (A collection of symbolical folk songs of the Karbis), **Dampijuk Chingdi** (A collection of modern poems of different Karbi poets), **Jutang Amung** (A collection of essays on Karbi cultures and traditions written by different writers). **Adamasar** (the marriage system of the Karbis), and other Karbi textbooks for primary schools.

Under Publication

Sengve (A collection of poems), **Pirthe Keplang** (the origin of the earth according to the Karbi mythology), **Jangreso** (The story of the stranger hero in the Karbi folk story), **Rupat Chethi** (Karbi Short stories), **Atur Kemi** (A Karbi novel which was serialised in **Manjir** magazine).

Contact Information

Bidor Sing Kro
Rongthe-ang,
P.O. : Diphu-0782460
Distt.: Karbi Anglong (Assam),
Phone : 03671-73522 (R)

BONGLONG TERANG

Personal

Bonglong Terang was born in 1909 in Dillai Porbat. His father, Terang, was a prominent social leader. His mother, Kareng Tissopi, was a housewife. He died in 1997.

Education

Terang was educated at Golaghat in the district of Sibsagar of Assam, but he left school before completing his education.

Contribution

Bonglong Terang, was a Karbi writer. He travelled widely in Assam, studying various festivals and documenting a rich heritage of Karbi folk songs and folklore. Terang wrote mostly on Karbi customs. However he also made important contributions to Karbi law and justice, collecting some important documents relating to these issues. Three of his books have been published.

Selected Published Works

Adam Asar (Marriage Law)—1936, **Rukasen**—1936, **Ha-I**—1936, *Karbi Kopuson*, *Karbi Aren Ateng* and *Ronglin*, *Tiput*, and *Karbi Chorangji*.

HANG MIJI HANSE

Personal

Hang Miji Hanse was born on December 22, 1962. He is a member of the Karbi tribe. He lives in Hongkram in the Karbi Anglong Distrtict of Assam. Hanse is a government servant.

Education

Hanse graduated with a degree in Mechanical Engineering.

Contribution

Hanse writes in Karbi, Assamese and English. A poet and short story writer, Hanse has published two books. He is currently compiling a **History of the Karbi Tribe.**

Selected Published Works

Plipli Nenipru—1990, and **Longchapsarpo**—2001.

Contact Information

Hang Miji Hanse
79, Hong Kram
At & P.O. : Hong Kram
Pin : 782450
Distt : Karbi Anglong,
(Assam)

JOHN TIMUNG

Personal

John Timung was born on January 1, 1958 at Listore ponk Amo Kom under Sojong, Distt. Karbi Anglong. Presently a priest in St. Thomas Church, Hidipi in Karbi Anglong District of Assam. Shri Timung is also engaged in teaching and music.

Education

B.A. from Anthony's College, Shillong, M.A. in Theology from North-East University, Shillong. He is also post-graduate from Rome in Italy.

Contribution

John Timung's field of literery activity is chiefly essays and translation. His published works include six books, the first, titled **Arnam Alam** was published in 1990. He has also been editing the Karbi monthly, **Samphri Atur** since 1993.

Selected Published Works

Hemphu Arni Kardom Kardi Aron (1994), **Sining Atovar** (2000), **Adam Asar Aron** (2002) and **Guitar Kardeng Kacharli** (Kitab-1).

Contact Information

John Timung
Bishaps House
P.O. : Diphu,
Distt. : Karbi Anglong-782460
(Assam)
Telephone : 03675-213158

LONGKON TERON

Personal

Longkon Teron was born in 1936 at Dokmoka, which was then in the Nowgaong District of Assam. His father was Diplu Teron and his mother was Sangpi Kachai Hansepi.

Longkon Teron is remembered as one of the greatest sons of the Karbi community. After teaching for some years and being Headmaster of Dokmoka, M.E. School, he became a public relations officer under the District Council and earned a reputation for being a sincere and honest officer. He was General Secretary and later President of the Karbi Adorbar organisation. He was elected President of the Karbi Lomment Amei in 1966.

Education

Longkon received schooling only up to high school at Kampur High School, Dokmoka, as some compelling family problems prevented him from continuing his education.

Contribution

Most of Longkon's writing is related to the Karbi language. Among his published works are **Rongke Song** (Formation of Model) and **Sar Lamthe** (Karbi Phrases and Idioms). He also wrote educational textbooks for primary classes and made a significant contribution as Secretary of the Karbi Textbook Committee. He was Vice-President of the Assom Sahitya Sabha.

Selected Published Works

Rongke Song (Formation of Model) and **Sar Lamthe** (Karbi Phrases and Idioms), **Tam Hidi** (Ka Kha), **Danpicjuk** (class A), **Kitab Limi (I, II, III)**. **Lam Majong** (class A), **Karbi Tanagurthi.**

Contact Information

Longkon Teron
C/o The Karbi Anglong Bus Association
P.O. : Diphu : 782460
Distt. : Karbi Anglong
(Assam)
Telephone : 03671-273942 (R)

LUNSE TIMUNG

Personal

Lunse Timung was born in 1942 at Dillowjan Don Timung village in the Sibsagar District of Assam. His parents were Kania Timung and Kajor Terangpi.

When he was barely four years old, he suffered the bereavement of his mother. At the beginning of his career he was a teacher, first in a primary school and later in M.E. School, Chokihola. He then became Assistant Sub-Inspector of Schools under the Karbi Anglong District Council. In 1978 he resigned from this job and joined politics, eventually serving for two terms as a member of the District Council. He has also been active in social organisations. He was President of the **Karbi Riso Adorbar** (Karbi Youth Organisation) and also General Secretary of the Karbi Adorbar. In 1997 he was elected Vice-President of the **Karbi Lamment Aamei**. He was elected President of the Karbi Lamment Aamei in 1999 and again in 2001.

Education

Timung began his schooling at the age of six. After his primary education he was admitted to Sarihajan Seva Kendra, a branch of the Adivasi Seva Samiti, Rajasthan, where he passed his high school examination in 1963. He attended Devraj Roy College, Golaghat, but eventually he left this college and completed Pre-University and BA Part-I at Diphu College, Diphu in 1968 and 1970, respectively.

Contribution

Lunse Timung writes on social issues. He is well-known for his books on social and customary laws. He has also edited several educational textbooks.

Selected Published Works

Thoi Kiri Hojong Recho—2005, **Karbi Aron Ajutang** (Customary

Law)—1999, **Choti Chotor** (Social Code) and **Kanbala Kambata** (Traditional Faith).

Contact Information

Lunse Timung
Village/City : Luru Langso
P.O. : Diphu - 782460
Distt. : Karbi Anglong
(Assam)

DR. PHUKAN CH. PHANGCHO

Personal

Dr. Phukan Ch. Phangcho was born in a middle class peasant family of the Karbi tribe on October 31, 1946. He was born in Panbari village in the Kamrup District of Assam. He writes mostly essays in both Assamese and English. He lives in Dongkamukam, in the Karbi Anglong District of Assam, with his wife, a teacher at a local high school, three college-going sons, and his elderly mother. Presently he is the principal of Rangsina college.

In 1998 Phangcho was honoured as an educator by the District administration, on the occasion of Golden Jubilee of India's Independence. He is also a recipient of the **Best Citizen of India** Award given by the International Publishing House (1999).

Education

Phangcho received his primary education in his native village. For secondary and higher education he moved to Guwahati. After completing an M.Sc. in 1971, he moved to Shillong to teach geography at a college. He received his Ph.D. in 1990.

Contribution

Phangcho has five published books to his credit. A number of his articles, mostly research articles, have appeared in both English and Assamese journals. He is also a singer and painter. Exhibitions of his paintings on Karbi folk art and culture have been held both at the district and state levels. His paintings are also displayed in the Shankardev Kalakshetra Art Gallery, Guwahati.

He is the founder of the Assam Science Society of Ronkhang Branch and the Karbi Anglong College Principals Council. He has also been the President of Karbi Anglong Dist. Sahitya Sabha and member of District Education Council.

Selected Published Works

The Karbis of North-East India (English)—2003, **Sabin Alun** (English translation of Karbi Ramayana)—2002, **Karbi Anglong and North Cachar Hills** (English)—2001, **Prabandha Sankalan** (Assamese and English)—2000, **Prakriti Aru Manuh** (Assamese)—1999.

Contact Information

Phukan Ch. Phangcho
House No. : 45/TC, Dongkamukam
Distt. : Karbi Anglong : 782485 (Assam)

PORESH CHANDRA RONGPHAR

Personal

Poresh Chandra Rongphar was born to a Karbi Tribal family on January14, 1932 in Porojan, in the east Mikhir hills near Sibasagar District in Assam. He joined government service in 1972. He writes under the pen name **Tung'e Longkumar**.

Education

Rongphar briefly attended Duboroui L P School at the age of 12, but was forced to discontinue his studies because of the Japanese invasion during the Second World War. However, he was able to rejoin the same school in 1946. He joined Golaghat Town High School in 1961 and matriculated from Sarihajan High School in 1965.

Contribution

In 1961 Rongphar started writing poems, short stories and novels in Karbi. Till now he has published only one book of poetry in Karbi. Rongphar was awarded by the **Karbi Sahitya Sabha** in 1998.

Selected Published Works

Vorali Ahir—1999.

Contact Information

Poresh Chandra Rongphar
Near T.V. Centre
Village : Chiphongchingri
P.O. : Disama
Distt. : Karbi Anglong, Pin : 782460, (Assam)
Telephone: 03671-274115 (O) / 03671-75482 (R)

RONGBONG ENGTI KATHAR

Personal

Rongbong Engti Kathar was born on March 1, 1946. His father, the late Hemari Engti Kathar, was a member of the Karbi tribe living in the plains. Kathar is a teacher at Barboha High School and presently resides in Barboha Karbi village, in the Nagaon District of Assam.

Education

Kathar is a B.A. from Nagaon College under Gauhati University.

Contribution

Kathar's work has been published in various magazines and newspapers and includes poems, short stories, dramas, and essays in Karbi and Assamese. He has three books: one poetry collection, one autobiography and one book in the Karbi language which have been published so far. Kathar was the editor of three yearly magazines: **Owekimi** (1967), **Smaranika** (1990), and **Shikhayabrati** (1992). His talks on educational, social and cultural issues have been broadcast in Karbi by All India Radio, Guwahati.

He has been awarded a certificate by the **Karbi Lammet Amei** (Karbi Sahitya Sabha), Diphu in honour of his literary contributions.

Selected Published Works

Bhinasur (a collection of poems)—1982, **Shikhar Bonty Nila Kanta Borkakaty** (an autobiographical work)—1982, **Alam Charlinang** (in Karbi)—1997.

Contact Information

Rongbong Engti Kathar
No. : 6, Borboha Karbi Goan,
At & P.O. : Borboha,
Dist. : Nagaon, Pin : 782445, (Assam)
Telephone : 284067 (R) 284144 (O)

RONGBONG TERANG

Personal

Born in a Karbi family, Rong Bong Terang is an important writer of Assam. Rongbong Terang is an eminent Karbi novelist and short story writer of Assam. He writes in Assames Language. He was Professor in Diphu Government College from where he entired.

Education

He is an M.A. in Assamees.

Contribution

He wrote Karbi folk tales in Assamese language. He has some important important translation works to his credit. Karbi translation of **Srimad Bhagvat Geeta** is one such work. He was awarded Padma Shri Award on his book **Rongmillir Khanki.**

Selected Published Works

Rongmilir hanhi (Assamese novel), **Rongmili ki muskan** (Hindi version of Rongmilir hanhi), **Kranti kalor ashru** (Assamese novel), **Ban pharingar geet** (Assamese novel), **Karbi sahitya sanskritir abhumuki** (Assamese essays), **Neela orchid** (Assamese short story), **Karbi sadhu** (Karbi folk-tales written in Assamese), **Karbi asomiya path** (Text book), **Dola alun** (Karbi folk song), **Ne lun ne lamthe** (Collection of poems written by late kanam Hansepi), **Shrimadbhagavat Geeta** (Geeta, translated into Karbi), **Karbi lamtasam** (A pocket dictionary of the Karbis)

Contact Information

Rongbong Terang
Rong mong, Chana Road,
Opposite Law College, Diphu
Pin : 782460 (Assam)
Telephone : 03671-273293

SEMSONSING INGTI

Personal

Semsonsing Ingti was born in 1923 in Golaghat in the Sibsagar District of Assam. His father, Thengkursing Ingti, lived at Mission Compound, Golaghat. After some years of teaching in a high school he became Sub-Inspector of Schools. During his service career he travelled widely in Assam and encouraged the Karbi people to adapt themselves to modern life. In 1945 he resigned from this job and joined the Karbi Adorbar as its General Secretary. He is remembered for making an important contribution during his association with this organisation. He led the movement for the creation of a separate Karbi District, which resulted in the creation of United Mikir and North Cachar Hills Districts in 1951. Although the district was finally renamed the Karbi Anglong Autonomous District in 1974. Semsonsing Ingti did not live to see his dream fulfilled. He died in 1948 at the young age of 35. His death was a great loss to the Karbi society.

Education

Ingti received his early education in Golaghat. After doing Intermediate in Arts from Cotton College, Guwahati, he was admitted to Murari Chand College, Sylhit, where he completed his B.A.

Contribution

Semsonsing Ingti was a short story writer who wrote fiction with the aim of instilling the spirit of learning and education in the Karbi people. He is known for his works on short stories in the Karbi language. He has published four books.

Selected Published Works

Bituso, Tomo Puru, KalaUha and Osomar Ascitap (all books of short stories).

CHARU MOHAN RABHA

Personal

Charu Mohan Rabha was born on February 25, 1954 in Chatabari under the Lakhipur Police Station in the district of Goalpara in Assam. His childhood was very difficult as his father, the late Kaltu Ram Rabha and mother, Kafeng Bala Rabha were poor and illiterate. He writes both prose and poetry. He presently works in the Department of Electricity (ASEB) in Assam as an AAO in the Dhupdhara Electrical Sub-Division.

Education

Rabha did his early schooling at the village Lower Primary School and Baida M.V. School. He did his matriculation from Nehru Vidyapeeth High School in 1972. He could not continue his college education as a regular student. As a private student he completed his B.A. in Astrology in 1988 from the Institute of Astrological Research Project, Kolkata.

Contribution

Rabha has been writing since he was a student in primary school. His poems and essays have appeared in different Assamese and Rabha magazines and newspapers. Two of his books **Goalparia Sanskritir Dukharia Chabi** and **Rabha Kramichi Rubung Chak**, are currently under print. Besides these, Assamese-Rabha-Laxicon is ready for publication. About one hundred articles of Charu Mohan Rabha have been published in various magazines.

Rabha is the president of Mechpara Madhyanchal Rabha Samaj, Baida since 2000 and was the Joint Secretary of the All Rabha Literary Society (Bebak Rabha Khraurang Runchum).

In 1999 he was honoured as a **Jyotish Vachaspati** by the Astro-Guide, Barasat, Kolkata.

Selected Published Works

Monimala—2003, Rabha Krau-michini Halsa—2000, Rabha Sanskritir Chamu Parichay—2000, Khusumbrip Paar—1998, Rabha Bir Dadan Maru Khetri—1997.

Contact Information

Charu Mohan Rabha
House No. : 33, Villege : Chatabari,
P.O. : Jurigaon,
Distt : Goalpara-783120, (Assam)

UPEN RABHA HAKACHAM

Personal

Upen Rabha Hakacham was born on January 8, 1963 in a Rabha tribal family in Chatabari village in the Goalpara District of Assam. He writes poetry, drama and fiction in Rabha, his tribal language. Hakacham started teaching while he was still a student. He taught science in a school for two years. He also worked for six years as an officer-in-charge at the Directorate of Museums, Assam. In 1992 he returned to teaching and joined Gauhati University as a lecturer in Assamese. Presently, he is the Reader in the same university. He is the only person who speaks Maitori, a sub-group of Rabha language, to reach such a high position in academia.

Education

Hakacham received his primary education from village schools. He matriculated from Boida High School and graduated from B.P.C. College, Nagarbera in 1984. He completed his post-graduation from Gauhati University in 1988. He received a Ph.D. from the same university for his research entitled, **Rabha and Assamese Language: A Comparative Study.**

Contribution

Hakacham started writing when he was still a student. Nearly two hundred articles on topics related to his tribal language, literature and culture have been published in different Assamese and English magazines and news bulletins. He has also written two dramas in the Rabha language and two books for the university curriculum in Assamese. He has edited two books of nursery rhymes and Indian tales. His compilation of a dictionary and a preparation of grammerr for the University Grants Commission is also a significant contribution.Two books co-authored by him titled **A Typological Grammer of Rabha and Rabha-Assamese-English Dictionary are to be published soon by ABILAC.**

Selected Published Works

In Rabha: Edited

Song-hasangini Khircha (translation of Indian tales)—2000, **Ranggir Parsuram** (drama)—1998, **Mamorangi Mayna Khurang** (nursery rhymes) —1997, **Sati Dyumakchi** (drama)—1987.

In Assamese

Asamiya Aru Asamar Tibbat- Boroniya Bhasa (linguistics)—2000, **Rabha Bhasa Aru Sahitya** (collection of articles relating to the Rabha language)—1997, **Asom Sahitya Sabha Patrika** (anthology of Rabha poetry)—1997, **Rabha Byakaram, Vol. II** (Rabha grammar)—1993/ 1998.

In English

Co-authored, Languages of the North-East—1997.

Contact Information

Upen Rabha Hakacham
Reader, University Campus,
Gauhati University,
Kamrup : 781014 (Assam)
Telephone : 0361-2573320
E-mail : rabhaupen@rediffmail.com

SANDESH BAKSHAKA

Personal

Sandesh Bakshaka was born on June 18, 1961 in Meghalaya. He is a member of the Rabha Tribe. He is currently a teacher.

Education

Bakshaka is doing his BA from IGNOU. He holds a **Visharad** in Hindi under the Assam Rastrya Bhasa Prachar Samiti, Guwahati.

Contribution

Bakshaka has been producing Rabha literary works since 1978, and has been helping the All Rabha Sahitya Sabha. He is a poet, novelist, short story writer, dramatist, artist, and painter. He writes in Rabha, Assamese and Hindi. He also composes songs and lyrics in Rabha and performs Rabha modern songs on All India Radio, Tura. Bakshaka's published works include two books.

Selected Published Works

Hasongi Parchung (Rabha poetry)—2002, **Orihong**—1996, **Bingbrat** (a magazine).

Contact Information

Sandesh Bakshaka
Nill 8,
P.O. : Photamati,
District : West Garo Hills,
Meghalaya : 794109

PRITHIVI MAJHI

Personal

Prithivi Majhi was born on January 24, 1951 in Baughpara Tea Estate in Assam. His father was the late Birsing Majhi and his mother is Sita Majhi. He is married to Tarulata Kakoti Majhi, and they have two daughters and two sons. At present he is Speaker of Assam Legislative Assembly.

Education

Majhi received his B.A. from DHSK College in Dibrugarh and his LL.B. from Dispur Law College at Gauhati University.

Contributions

He is particularly recognized for having compiled an important Dictionary of Santali, Assamese and English. Majhi has written several articles which have been published in several different magazines and newspapers. In addition to being associated with many literary, cultural, and social organisations at the state and national levels, Majhi was awarded an Honorary Membership in the All India Santali Writers Association.

He has also served in many governmental positions, and was elected Member of the Legislative Assembly from 117-Lahowal constituency in 1996 and again in 2001. He also served as a Member of Parliament from 1984, 1990.

In his educational roles, Majhi served as President, North East Regional Institute of Parliamentary Studies, Training and Research in Khanapara, Guwahati. He also served as the secretary of the Assam Tea Garden Tribes Students Asociation from 1968, 1978 and is the General Secretary of the All Assam Santal Committee.

Majhi has travelled extensively abroad including to Geneva to attend the 17th Session of the Working Group of Indigenous Populations Conference at the United Nations. He also attended the 48th, 49th, and 50th Conference of the CPA in Australia, Bangladesh, and Canada, respectively.

Selected Published Works

Santal-Assamese-English Dictionary (Under Publication).

Contact Information

Prithivi Majhi
Speaker, Assam Legislative Assembly
Dispur, Guwahati (Assam)

BIREN BORDOLOI

Personal

Biren Bordoloi was born on January 27, 1973. He is a member of the Tiwa tribe. He works as a teacher at a high school.

Education

Bordoloi has a university degree in science.

Contributions

Bordoloi is a poet and writes in the Tiwa tribal language as well as Assamese, English and Hindi. Bordoloi's poems have been published in several magazines, including **Saptarkhi.**

Contact Information

Biren Bordoloi
Sankar Dev Nagar, Jorapukhuri
Distt. : Nagaon (Assam)
Pin : 782446
Telephone : (pp) 03674-284017

RAJENDRA NATH BORDOLOI

Personal

Rajendra Nath Bordoloi was born in the Lalung community of the Tiwa tribe. He speaks and writes principally in Assamese. He currently lives in Ambikagiri Nagar, Guwahati and works in government service.

Education

Bordoloi received his B.A. He has also passed the Praveen, the highest exam of the Asom Rashtra Bhasa Samhiti in Guwahati, Assam.

Contributions

Bordoloi is a poet, short story writer, critic, and essayist. He writes in both Assamese and Hindi. Bordoloi has published three collections of his own poetry and has also edited three anthologies of poems.

Selected Published Works

Punashwa—1999, **Kabita Barshikee**—1997, **Matir Premat Manuh**—1992, **Prabahita Samay**—1987, **Urbar Bhumit**—1984, **and Kanthaswar**—1981 He has also edited three anthologies of poems.

Contact Information

Rajnedra Nath Bordoloi
Amibika Giri Nagar, Guwahati,
P.O. : Zoo Road, Distt. : Kamrup (Assam)
Pin : 781024
Telephone : 2206900 (R)
Mo. : 09435047675

Manipur

Paite/Tangkhul

DR. T.S. GANGTE

Introduction

Dr. T.S. Gangte is about 66 years (Age as on 1-2-2004) old. He belongs to the Gangte Tribe of Manipur. He has pioneered in the promotion of Higher Education in the Hill Areas among the backward tribal people in North-East. He contributed as Director, Chairman, members, Vice-President, Life Time members in the State and Central Govt. Institutions, Organisations, Commissions etc.

Education

— M.A. in Sociology (Delhi School of Economics), University of Delhi.
— Ph.D. in Anthropology (A), University of Calcutta.

Contributions

He has been the founder Principal, Churachandpur Government College, Manipur, for 23 years. He was, then, promoted to Director of Education (University and Higher Education), Government of Manipur for 5 years.

Publications

— A book on "The Kukis of Manipur", 1993.
— A book on "Nehru and North-East India", 1993.
— A book on "A Century of Government and Politics in the North-East India, Vol. IV; Manipur 1991.
— A book on "Anglo-Kuki War 1917-1919".
— "Why Must We Be Mizo, 2005".

Contact Information

Former Director of Education, New Tambu Lane, Imphal-1.

CHIHANPAM SAREO

Personal

Chihanpam Sareo (Tangkhul Naga) was born on September 12, 1945. He is the eldest of eleven children. His father worked as the headmaster in a government primary school. In 1966 Sareo joined as an assistant matriculation teacher in a government middle school. At present he is serving as a lecturer of **Tangkhul Language** in the Ukhrul Higher Secondery School, Manipur.

Education

Sareo completed his elementary education in the Ukhrul District of Manipur. He then moved to St. Anthony High School, Shillong, but passed his matriculation at a different school in Imphal in 1966. He eventually passed pre-university from Pettigrew College, Manipur.

Contribution

Sareo has prepared several books in Tangkhul Naga Language for teaching in Schools. Chihanpam Sareo wrote textbooks for the second, third, tenth and twelfth standards.

He has served as a member of the Tangkhul Literary Society. The tribal language Tangkhul was recognized by the State Government of Manipur as a medium for education in 1985. He has been directed by Manipur University to prepare the manuscript of T.D.C. in Tangkhul Language to be implemented in the academic session in 2005.

He was given **Rajkumari Sanatompi Award** on September 5th, 1995 by the Manipur State Government.

Selected Published Works

Textbooks of the Tangkhul Naga language for Classes II, III, X and XII.

Contact Information

Chihanpam Sareo
Awungtang, Near Savio School,
Ukhrul : 795142, (Manipur)

H. KAMKHENTHANG

Personal

H. Kamkhenthang was born on March 1, 1949 in Manipur. His father was the late Reverend Taivel. He is a member of the Paite community. He is currently the Joint Director (TRI) of the Directorate for Development of Tribals and Scheduled Castes, Government of Manipur.

Education

Kamkhenthang is an M.Sc. and Ph.D. in **Social Anthropology.**

Contribution

Kamkhenthang is Poet, Story writer & Essayist. Besides this, he is a Translator and Journalist. He has witten as well as translated many books. He has edited and co-edited many Journals and Magazines.

Kamkhenthang has been published in numerous academic and literary journals. He has also served as the editor of **Zougam Zunna,** an annual research journal written in Paite language, for several years.

Kamkhenthang was a member of the General Council of Manipur State Kala Akademi for three terms. He was a member of the Executive Body of the Manipur State Kala Akademi for two terms. He is a life member of the North East India Council for Social Sciences Research, Shillong. He is also the member of the Board of Directors of the Paite Literature Society, the North East Zonal Cultural Centres of Kolkata and Dimapur, the Advisory Board of the Adimjati Shiksha Ashram, Manipur for two terms and has served as secretary and chairman in various expert committees appointed by the State Government.

Selected Published Works

Book In Paite (Tedim Chin)

English-Paite (Tedim)—1983, **Lapau** (A dictionary of poetical words)—1990, **Paite Paunak** (Paite Proverbs explained in social cultural context)—1993, **Zaila Sak louh Zaila** (Social songs), **Zoulai**

Gelhdan (Rules for Writing Paite)—1999, **Tuun Leh Zua** (Reminiscence of Parents by siblings)—2000, **Thu Leh La** (A Textbook of Prose and Poetry for Classes IX & X)—1988, **Siamsil Thaikawi** (Paite Rapid Reader for Class IX)—1997, **Siamsil Tongsan** (Paite Language Paper for Classes XI & XII)—2000, **Pau leh Lai Gelhdan** (Grammar & Composition for Classes IX & X)—2000.

H. Kamkhenthang translated the following books into Paite language:

Madhabi (First Manipuri novel of Kamal Singh)—1983, **Genevieve Thangthu** (by C. Schmidt)—1982, **Tate Etkolna Panpithtu** (Nurturing of Children) 1982, **Khamtheili Goih Ka hi** (I was a Drug Addict by Ravinder Singh, into Chingzaman, Imphal), **Gamtate Omdan Hoih** (book of Watson, E. into Paite)—2002.

Co-authored, Goswami, M.C. and Kamkhenthang, H. "Mother's Brother in Paite Society", *Bulletin of the Department of Anthropology*, Guahati University, Vol. No. 1, 1971. "Uterine Brothers and Sisters" (Laizom) Among the Paite, *Journal of the University of Guwahati*, Vol. XX-XXII No. 2 Sciene 1969-71. "Nicotine Habit of the Paite", *Bulletin of the Department of Anthropology*, Guahati University Vol. No. III, 1974. "Paite Dwelling House", *Bulletin of the Department of Anthropology*, Guahati University, Vol. No. V, 1976. "Ritual Experts (Siampi) Among the Paite", *Bulletin of the Department of Anthropology*, Guahati University Vol. V, 1976.

Co-authored, Thuamson, H. & Kamkhenthang, H. *The Paite,* Quarterly Journal of the Manipur State Kala Akedemi, Vol. II No. I, 1977. *The Tarao,* Quarterly Journal of the Manipur State Kala Akademi, Imphal Vol. II No. I, 1983. *The Social and Political Institution of the Paite,* (Edited by Yayanta Sarkar and B. Datta Ray) Social and Political Institutions of the Hill People of North East India, 1990, Calcutta Anthropological Surevey of India . *Religion of the Northern Chins* (Zoomi) Religions of the Tribes of North East India, 1984, Vendrame Missiological Institute, Shillong. *Features of Paite Folklore,* Quarterly Journal of the Manipur State Kala Akademi Vol. IV No.2, 1986.

Co-authored, Roy, A.K & Kamkhenthang, H. *The Trend of Shifting Cultivation in Manipur and its Control,* Shifting Cultivation in North East India, Edited by D.N. Majumdar, Omson Pulications, New Delhi. *District Council in Manipur Vis-a-vis the Sixth Schedule and a Note on Draft on Modality,* 1997, Autonomous District Council (Edited by L.S Gassh Omson Publications, New Delhi).

Co-authored, Kamkhenthang, H. *Lamka* (Churachandpur) Town, Urban Development in North-East India (Potentiality and Problems), 1998, Edited by B. Datta Ray et al, Reliance Publishing House, Delhi. *Zoumi-Mizo Continuum,* 1995, Manipur Past and Present Vol. III (Edited by N. Sanajaoba), Mittal Publications, Delhi. *The Paite,* People of India, Manipur Volume, Anthropological Survey of India, New Delhi. *Vaiphei* People of India, Manipur Volume, Anthropological Survey of India, New Delhi. *The Thadou* People of India, Manipur Volume, Anthropological Survey of India, New Delhi. *Folk Tales of Moyon-Monsang,* 1982, Imphal, Directorate for Development of Tribals and Backward Classes, Government of Manipur. *Maram Folktales,* 1985, Imphal, Directorate for Development of Tribals and Backward Classes, Government of Manipur. *The Paite, A Transborder Tribe of India and Burma,* 1986, Mittal Publications, New Delhi. *Groping For Identity,* 1986, in Search of Identity (Edited by Kamkhenthang et al), Kuki-Chin Baptist Union, Imphal.

Co-authored, Jamkhothang, T. & Kamkhenthang, H. *A Brief Introduction to the Language and Culture of the Paite (Tedim Chin),* 1976, Introduction to Tribal Languages and Culture of Manipur (7 Tribes) Edited by Dr. K.B. Singh Manipur State Kala Akademi, Imphal.

Contact Information

H. Kamkhenthang
Present Address : Paite-veng,
Kwakeithel, Imphal 795001, Manipur
Permanet Address : Upper Lamka,
Tuipaimukh Road, Manipur
Telephone : 0385-2455224/0385-2455325
email : hoihnu hauzel<hhauzel@yahoo.co.in>

ROBIN S. NGANGOM

Personal

Ngangom was born in January, 1959. A poet, story writer, editor and translator, he also currently teaches as a lecturer in the Department of English, NEHU.

Education

Ngangom did his BA in English from St. Edmund's College in Shillong in 1981, and his M.A. in English from NEHU in 1983. He subsequently worked as a lecturer at St. Edmund's College from 1986 to 1988 when he accepted his current post as a lecturer at NEHU.

Contributions

Besides teaching, Ngangom is also the editor for **New Frontiers,** the journal of the Northeast Writer's Forum, Guwahati. He is also the nominating editor for Manipuri for the translation awards, KATHA, New Delhi. He himself was awarded the **KATHA Award** for Translation in 1999. He was also invited to participate in the UK Year of Literature and Writing, 1995, and received the **Udaya Bharati National Award** for Poetry in 1994 and 3rd prize in the Vineet Gupta Memorial Poetry Contest, 1987. Ngangom has published in several poetry anthologies and individual pieces in various magazines and journals such as—**The Telegraph Colour Magzine** (Kolkata), **Debonier** (Mumbai), **Contemporary Indian Literature** (Sahitya Academy) and **New Statesman** and **Society** (London).

Selected Published Works

Anthology of Contemporary Poetry from the Northeast (NEHU Publications)—2003, **A New Book of Indian Poems in English** (Writers Workshop, Calcutta)—2000, **Khasia in Gwalia** (Alun Books)—1995, **Time's Crossroads** (Disha Books)—1994, **An Anthology of New Indian English Poetry** (Rupa & Co)—1993, **Words and the Silence** (Writer's Workshop, Kolkata)—1988.

Contact Information

Robin S. Ngangom
House No. 49, NEHU Campus
Mawkynroh : Umshing, Shillong : 793 022
Meghalaya, INDIA
Telephone : 2723513 (O), 2551652 (R)
Email : robinngangom@yahoo.co.in

Meghalaya

Khasi

BEWAN LIONEL SWER

Personal

Bewan Lionel Swer is an essayist, folklorist and critique of Khasi literature. Presently, he is a Professor in the Department of Khasi, NEHU. He first joined Synod College, Shillong and then in 1982 moved to Khasi Department, NEHU. He was the first regular lecturer in this department. He is also the Chairman, Programme of Folklore Research and Archives, NEHU and a co-ordinator of the Entrepreneur Development Cell, NEHU. He was also the Member of the Board of Directors, YMCA, Shillong.

In addition to the above, he was associated with several organizations in various capacities, viz., President, Shillong College Governing Body (1973—94), President, Seng Khasi College(1982), President, Shillong Law College (1987—91), Life Member Indian Red Cross Society (1980), President, Seng Khasi (1984—95), President Sein Jainta (1977—84), President, Managing Committee, Ramkrishna Mission, Shillong (1986), President, Managing Committee, Ramkrishna High School, Sohra (1989— till date), etc. State Council of Bharat Scouts and Guides, Meghalaya (from 1884— till date).

Education

M.A., B.T. Ph.D.

Contribution

Swer has published a number of books of wide ranging variety such as criticism on almost all genres of writing, collection of poems and folkloristics. He also translated some Khasi books into English. Works of Swer are either texts or references for college and universities as well as research scholars. Swer was invited by the Welsh Academy, Cardiff, Wales for a three week residency under Khasi Welsh Writer's Exchange programme. There he actively participated in a number of talks, poetry readings and interactions.

He has been President, Khasi Authors' Society (1982-84), Convenor, Meghalaya Chapter of the Indian National Trust for Art & Cultural Heritage (1985—91), Member, Governing Body North-East Zone Cultural Centre, Dimapur (1986-92), Life Member, North-East India Council for Social Science Research (1986), He was also Chief Organiser and Editor of the Khasi Humourous Society and Editor of the Hynniewtrep Endeavour Society.

He received in 1999 the **State Literary Award for** the year 1997—98 for his books **Na Pneli Ka Rynsan** (a critique on drama) and **Ka Mationg Ki Khanatang** (a study of Khasi folk tales).

Selected Published Works

Na Pneli Ka Rynsan, Ka Matong Ki Khantong

Contact Information

Bewan Lionel Swer C/o Ms. Mebalazer S. Shullai, M.Sc. B.Ed., Mission Compound, Maukhar, Shillong-793002, Meghalaya Telephone : 03642545575

BIJOYA SAWIAN

Personal

Bijoya Sawian was born on November 15, 1949 in Shillong (Meghalaya). Her mother is a member of the Khasi tribe and her father is from Bengal. She married Alark Singh, who is from Himachal Pradesh, in 1974.

Education

Sawian passed her intermediate exams from Loreto Convent, Shillong, in 1966. In 1967 she joined Lady Sri Ram College, University of Delhi, and graduated in English, with Honors, in 1970. She completed her post-graduation from Miranda House, University of Delhi, in 1972.

Contribution

Bijoya Sawian is a Story writer and Essayist. She works as a free-lance Journalist and Translator. Sawian has long been a regular contributor to magazines and newspapers. From the late 1970s to 1980s she wrote for **The Hindustan Times, The Times of India, Femina** and **Ilustrated Weekly of India**. She has also written travelogues, short stories and articles on Khasi culture. Sawian keeps busy doing independent research and presents papers at seminars and symposiums.

Sawian translated **Ka Jingsneng Tymmen,** a two-part compilation of Khasi etiquette and ethics, which was published in 1999 as **The Teachings of Elders.** Hers was the first translation of this book which was first published in Khasi. Her other book, a compilation of Khasi folk tales entitled **Khasi Folk Tales,** was published in 2002.

Sawian is presently translating another ancient book, **Ka Niam Wei U Blei** ("The Religion of One God"), and writing a work of fiction, tentatively titled **Men in the Shadows**, which focuses on the insurgency in the North-Eastern region of India and a collection of short stories.

Selected Published Works

The Teachings of Elders—2002, Khasi Folk Tales—1999, Crisis of Identity, Oral Tradition – The Personal Element and its Benefits.

Contact Information

Bijoya Sawian
Lakyrsiew II, Lower Mawprem, Shillong
Distt. : East Khasi Hills,
Meghalaya : 793002
Telephone : 0364-2547688, 2546094

B. PAKEM

Personal

B.Pakem was born in Jowai, Meghalaya in 1937. He was well known all over the country and even abroad. He began his academic career as a lecturer in Political Science at Union Christian College, Barapani. He then joined St. Edmund's College for one year, and from there moved to Dibrugarh University where he taught for seven years. During this period he was also a Research Fellow at the Indian School of International Studies, J.N.U., New Delhi. In 1974 he joined N.E.H.U. as Reader in the Department of Political Science. He also held the office of the Dean, School of Social Science at this university. He was active in politics, too and was elected in 1978 and 1983, a member of the Meghalaya Legislative Assembly. During these tenures he was a cabinet minister incharge of important portfolios like Education, Revenue and Agriculture. In December, 1991, he joined N.E.H.U. as its Vice-Chancellor. He was an Hony. Director of the I.C.S.S.R., N.E.R.C, Shillong and was also its Chairman. Earlier, he was also President of the North East Indian Council for Social Science Research, Shillong.

Education

Pakem had his school education at the Jowai Government High School. He graduated from St Anthony's College in 1959. He was awarded a gold medal in M.A.(Political Science) in 1963 in Gauhati University. He received a Ph.D. in 1972 from Dibrugarh University. Pakem also did LL.B. in 1965 from Guwahati Univerity.

Contribution

He wrote a number of books and contributed a very large number of original research papers, articles etc., published in different books and Journals. As a social scientist, he made significant contributions towards better appreciation of the problems of the people of the North Eastern region of India.

DESMOND L. KHARMAWPHLANG

Personal

Desmond L.Kharmawphlang was born on August 24th, 1964. He is presently a reader at North Eastern Hill University.

Education

Kharmawphlang is an M.A. and Ph.D. in English.

Contribution

Kharmawphlang is an eminent poet and short story writer. He writes in Khasi and English. He has also done a lot of documentation of Khasi folk songs and Khasi folklore. He has published three books.

Select Published Works

U Mawshanok, Here, Ki Matti Byrshaim.

Contact Information

Desmond L Kharmawphlang
Reader, English Dept.,
North East Hill University,
Shillong : 793022
Telephone : 0364-2231834(O)/ 0364-2548458(R)
Mobile : 9863060983, 9863061631

FILMECA MARBANIANG

Personal

Filmeca Marbaniang was born on March 12, 1979 in Mawkyrwat village in western Meghalaya. Her father is Smallford Syiemlieh and her mother Arphlinda Marbaniang. She is working as a lecturer at St. Anthony College, Shillong.

Education

Marbaniang is a graduate from Banasthali Vidyapith, Rajasthan. She was a gold medalist in post-graduation, which she completed at North East Hill University, Shillong. Filmeca is at present a research scholar at North East Hill University (NEHU), Shillong.

Contribution

Filmeca Marbaniang is a young Khasi poet and short story writer. She is keenly interested in collecting Khasi folk songs and folk Tales and translating them into Hindi. She writes in magazines.

Contact Information

Filmeca Marbaniang
C/o Mr. R. Lyngdoh,
Mawlai Kynton Massar, BL-C
Near Meseb Sub-Station
Shillong (Meghalaya)
Telephone : 0364-2550258

J. S. SHANGPLIANG

Personal

J.S. Shangpliang was born on March1, 1944 in a Khasi tribal family. Shangpliang has also been an NEHU guest lecturer.

Education

Shangpliang is an M.A. and Ph.D. The topic of his research was **Love as a Theme in Khasi Novels.** He was a Gold Medalist for the Master's Degree in 1985.

Contribution

Shangpliang writes both in Khasi and English. A versatile writer, he contributes to several genres including poetry, short story, drama, essay and criticism. Shangpliang has also had many articles and poems published in newspapers, literary magazines, and school and college magazines. He is the editor of the first Khasi digest and wrote the script for the first Khasi feature film, **I Meir Jong Nga**, (on Super-8) which was released in 1982.

Selected Published Works

Ki Snap Ka Novel (a collection of critical essays)—1991. **Leslie Hardinge Pde as a Novelist** (in English)—1988. **Ka Ri Umanam** (a five-act drama)—1984. **Ka Kitab Jingdhein Bathymmai**—1976. "Women in Khasi Literature" (a National Seminar Paper, NEHU), in **U Kritik**, Ed. S. S. Majaw.

Co-authored

Na kiwei bad Na Lade, Ha Ki Sngi Jong Ngi. Standardisation of Khasi Language.

Plays

Ka Kput, Tba la ka Langthohdoh, Iano Phin Kynnoh, Da Kumne

Pleng (a one-act play), **Pa Map ia U, Ka Apot i Pa, Sha Jinglaitluid** (Telecast through Shillong DDK).

Contact Information

J.S. Shangpliang
Lissie Cottage, Wahingdoh,
Shillong, East Khasi Hills District
Pin : 793001
(Meghalaya)
Telephone : 0364-2548364

JEEBON ROY

Personal

Babu Jeebon Roy was born in 1838 in Saitsohpen, Sohra Cherrapunji. His parents were U Ram Singh Korkata and Ka Tira Rani. He sought permission to establish a high school and dedicated his entire life to the cause of Khasi education after he heard the hurtful remark, **The Khasis have no brains. They do not need education beyond class 6.** He died on May 16th, 1903 at the age of sixty five.

Education

Jeebon Roy's formal education was through only the primary level since there was no higher level of education available in the Khasi hills at that period in the 19th century. But his father had received formal schooling in Kolkata and was fluent in Bengali; the experiences and knowledge he imparted to his son were instrumental in Jeebon Roy's informal education. Webster Davis Jyrwa has said of Roy, **Babu Jeebon Roy could have lived an easy life but, even at his young age, he preferred to spend his time in learning and in acquiring knowledge, whatever he could get from books and from whoever he came in contact.**

Contributions

In 1875, Babu Jeebon Roy began to petition the provincial and state governments to construct a Government High School in Shillong. Finding no governmental support, he began construction of a high school from his own funds in 1876, and the school was inaugurated in 1878. Eventually others came to understand the importance of such an educational institution and the Shillong Government High School was finally opened in 1880.

Babu Jeebon Roy's literary career began in 1895 when he published two volumes of the "Khasi Reader," both containing folk tales and ethical instruction. Next he wrote and published a History of India in Khasi. He used his knowledge of Sanskrit to produce Khasi adaptations of the Buddha Deb Charittra, Ramayana, and the Hitopadesa.

Jeebon Roy was particularly concerned about the protection and recording of Khasi religion and culture in the face of an increasing number of Christian missionary activities. Therefore he founded the Khasi cultural institution known as the Ka Seng Khasi in 1899. According to Webster Davis Jyrwa, "**Besides its main objectives to preserve the social, cultural traditional structure of the Khasis based on the fundamental principles laid down by the forefathers, it also contributed a lot towards the promotion of Khasi literature.**" To this end, Roy also founded the **Ri-Khasi Press** at Umsohsun in 1896 to publish Khasi books.

Selected Published Works

Hitopadesa—1898 (translation from Sanskrit), **Ramayana** — 1900 (translation from Sanskrit), **Chaitanya Charitra** — 1900 (translation from Sanskrit), **Buddha Deb Charitra** — 1901 (translation from Sanskrit), **Khasi Reader**, **History of India** (in Khasi) Shaphang U Wel U lel (About one God).

KITBOR W. NONGRUM

Personal

Kitbor W. Nongrum was born to W.S. Roy Thangkhiew and Konsila Nongrum on August 14, 1945. He is popularly known as Babu Kitbor. He belongs to the Khasi community. In 1966, at the age of 21, Nongrum started his career as a school teacher. He joined government service in the Meghalaya Secretariat in 1973 as an LDA, and finally, retired as the Under Secretary xfor Health and Family Welfare in 2002.

In the Social Services, he is the former Sector Warden, Secondary Field Management Committee, and the president of the youth organisation in the locality. He is the founder member of the **Khasi Author's Society, Study Tour Circle** and **SBUK** (Khasi Humourist Society). He is the former Secretary of the Managing Committee, Shon Roy Basan Secondary School. He is also the Elder of the Catholic church in the locality.

Education

In 1969 Nongrum was admitted to St. Anthony College, Shillong, with the intent of completing a Bachelor's Degree in Science. However he was unable to continue and left one year later. He later joined a different college and received a BA from Sankardev College, Shillong, in 1979.

Contribution

He started writing at a very young age. He is very versatile, being a novelist, dramatist, story writer, poet and singer. Kitbor has written extensively in his tribal language. He has also written material for the school curriculum. He has written and produced twelve novels, one short story book, two dramas, ten prose books, eight poetry collections, three nursery school books and four help books for schools. He also takes part in discussions, talks, recitation of self-composed poems, school programmes etc. in AIR, Shillong and also on Doordarshan Kendra, Shillong. He also participated in the North East Poet's Meet 1994 at Shillong organized by the NE Zone Cultural Centre, in a poetry reading 1995 organised by the Centre for Creative Arts, NEHU and also at the Regional Conference of All India Tribal Literary Forum in December, 2002 at Guwahati and was elected as a member of N.E. Regional Committee of AITLF.

He received The **North-Eastern Excellence Personalities Award,** 2003 from the International Penguin Publishing House, New Delhi; the **Meghalaya State Award,** 2002 **U Tirot Singh Award** for Arts and Literature; and the **Bharat Excellence Award** in 2000 from The Friendship Forum of India, New Delhi. He was also given a **Citation** as an author from Mondon Bareh Memorial, Shillong for his

Valuable Publications

Ki Nongthoh-Kot Khasi, Vol. I & II and Ki Kot Khubor Bad Ki Kot Khasi. He received the Meghalya Literary Award in 1983 for his novel Ka Jingiaishah.

Selected Published Works

Novels

U Bieit Bad Ka Khun U Patsha (selected by All India Radio Shillong for weekly programme "Novel Reading")—2002, **Ngan Ap Ia Phi** (selected by All India Radio Shillong for its weekly programme—"Novel Reading")—1999, **Nga Khlem Poi Pyrkhat**—1996, **Ka Biria Dei Por U Sbe Sing**—1992, **Nga Dang Kynamaw**—1991, **Balei Tang Ia I Thei?**—1988, **Ha Phi Nga Aiti**—1988, **Ka Jingieit Bajanal Ia Phi**—1987, **Nga Dang Ieit Ia Phi**—1987, **Ka Jingiaishah**–1983, **U Shanbor Bad U Wadbor**—1976, **Ka Pung Ka Jingieit**—1973.

Short Stories

Ki Ummat Jingieit—1987.

Drama

Ngam lah ban klet—1992, Ka Shatsngi—1991.

Prose

Ki Essay & Kiwei de—2001, Ka Jingtip Kyllum—2001, Nangne nangtai—1997, Ki Ktien shong sbai—1996, Ki Nongnoh-synniang sha ka Thoh ka Tar Khasi—1995, Katto Katne shaphang KI KOT DRAMA KHASI—1991, Ka Rukom shet Jingbam Khasi—1983, Ki Kot Khubor & Ki Kot Khasi—1982, Ki Nongthoh-kot Khasi Vol. II and II—1982.

Poetry

Ki Mawkordor ka iing ka sem—2002, Ki Matti u Khasi—2001, Kiba nga ñiewkor—2000, Ki Sur bat kpoh—1995, Hima Jingieit jong nga—1995, Ki Sur shong sbai—1994, Ki Sur ba dang sawa—1992, Ka Umpohliew—1982.

Contact Information

Kitbor W. Nongrum
4 ½ Mile, Upper Shillong
P.O. : Shillong, Meghalaya, Pin : 793005
Telephone : 0364-2560623 (R), (Mo.) : 09863061119

KYNPHAM SING NONGKYNRIH

Personal

Kynpham Sing Nongkynrih was born on April 4, 1964 in Cherrapunji, Meghalaya. He belongs to the Khasi tribe. Nongkynrih is Deputy Director, Publications, at North East Hill University (NEHU), Shillong. He is Canvenor of All India Tribal Literary Forum for Meghalaya Chapter and also a member of its Central Committee at the National lavel.

Education

Nongkynrih received Master's degree in English.

Contribution

Kynpham Sing writes poems and short stories in both Khasi and English. His widely published poetry, anthologised and researched is collected in two volumes in English and three in Khasi.

He has written sixteen books in Khasi and three in English. The Khasi books include three collections of poetry, one on practical criticism of poetry and two collections of amusing anecdotes published by local publishers. Nongkynrih's English books, including two collections of poetry from the Writers' Workshop in Calcutta and a collection of Khasi myths published by Allun Books in Wales, United Kingdom, are some of his important contributions to literature. Some of the poems from his forthcoming third collection have been included in the Indira Gandhi National Open University's new course for MA English titled **Contemporary Indian Literature in English Translation.** His poetry has also been researched by scholars in the Jawarharlal Nehru University, New Delhi and the Kakatiya University at Warangal in Andhra Pradesh. Nongkynrih has also translated ten National Book Trust publications into Khasi, some short stories from Khasi into English for **Katha,** as well as poetry and stories for the **Sahitya Akademi, New Delhi.** His first collection of folk-based short stories, **Death in a Hut and Other Stories from the Khasi Hills**, is being published by Alun Books, Wales, U.K.

Recently, he jointly edited the **first-ever Anthology of Contemporary Poetry from the Northeast,** published by him on behalf of NEHU. He edits the university newsletter, **NEHU News,** the university's official journal, The **NEHU Journal** and the first-ever poetry journal in Khasi, **Rilum.**

He received a **Consolation prize** from the American Poetry Associastion, Santa Cruz, in 1990. He was also awarded a publication grant from the Mehghalaya Government three times.

Selected Published Works

In English

Moments—(1992), **The Sieve**—(1992).

In Khasi

Ban Sngewthuh ia ka Piotri (a book of practical criticism on the understanding of poetry), **Ka Samoi jong ka Lyer** (Poetry), **Ki Mawsiang ka Sohra** (Poetry), **Ki Jingkynmaw** (Poetry).

Contact Information

Kynpham Sing Nongkynrih
Bijni Complex, NEHU, Shillong
Laitumkhrah, Distt.: East Khasi Hills, (Meghalaya) Pin : 793003
Telephone: 2211145 (R), 2226316, 2501902 (O)

MINIMON LALOO

Personal

Minimon Laloo was born on April 13, 1954 in Shillong in Jaintia tribe. She is continuously involved in social activities. She holds key posts in several organizations and associations working in Shillong. Laloo is Joint Secretary of the Meghalaya State Council for Child Welfare, Joint Secretary of her own Clan Society **Seng Kur Laloo**, and Joint Secretary of the Meghalaya branch of the **All India Tribal Literary Forum.** She is the Editor of the Khasi Authors Society. She is also a lifetime member of the All India Women Education Fund Association, Country Women Association of India and All India Poetess Conference.

Education

Laloo completed her schooling at St. Joseph Girls High School, Shillong. She graduated from Lady Keane Girls' College, Shillong, in 1974. She Passed DCE diploma from IGNOU in 1994.

Contribution

She is an author, regular radio artist, social worker and photographer. Laloo says about herself, **The year 1989 is a turning point in my life, I ventured into the world of literature through my first novel—** ***Tang Maphi Namar Jongnga.*** **Readers and prominent senior authors appreciated the flair I had for writing and encouraged me to continue writing.** She never stopped writing after this. She has written approximately twenty books in her tribal language, Khasi, as well as in English. She has also written novels, dramas, short stories, travelogues, humours and poetry. She is editor for the Khasi Authors', Society.

Selected Published Works

North-East General Knowldege and Sikkim (Revised and Enlarged)—2003, **Meghalaya—Land of Enchantment**—2000, **Ha Jylli ka Rynsan** (Drama)—2001, **Meghalaya Hand Book**—2001, **Sports and Games**—2000, **The North East General Knowledge New Millenium**—2000, **Wiat Rymmuin** (Humour)—1999, **Ka Lehniam ha Elaka Nartiang**—1997-98, **Ki Khana Lyngkot** (Short Stories for Children)—1996, **Shi Khung Ki Biria** (Humour)—1996, **Shano Ka Lawei u Hynniewtrep** (Drama)—1994, **Ki Biria u Shri Shdei** (Humorous)—1994, **Ka Thwei Lamin bad ka Lehniam Ki Pnar** (Indigeneous Rites of the Pnars)—1994, **Ai Ngan lap ha Ksangti Jongphi** (Romance)—1993, **Jar la ka Bhah** (Novel)—1992, **Our country and the world** (help book for class V as per NCERT syllabus)—1992, **Ki Sohkyrdot ka Jingieit** (Romance)—1991, **Ngam Banse** (Romance)—1990, **Tang Maphi Namar Jongnga** (Romance)—1989.

Contact Information

Minimon Laloo
C/o Mrs Bailin Syngkon, Mawkhar, Block-7
Shillong, East Khasi Hills, Meghalaya, Pin : 793001
Telephone : 2546566
(M) 98630-97146,
Fax : 0364-2503964, 2503958

Radhon Singh Berry Kharwanlang

Personal

Little was ever recorded about the birth and childhood of Radhon Singh Berry Kharwanlang, but it is known that he was born in Mawmluh (near Cherrapunjee) around 1850. It is also generally believed that he had, over the course of his life, two marriages and five children. He was a sensitive and reflective man who wrote beautiful songs for the Brahmo Samaj, the Seng Khasi, and the Unitarians. Progressive in thought and spirit, he practised the Khasi religion since birth and after studying Christianity for a few years, founded his own **Ka Niam U Wel U Blel**. He later joined this with the beliefs of Unitarian missionaries. He died when he was just over 50 years old.

Education

Very little is known about Radhon Singh Berry Kharwanlang's education.

Contributions

Radhon Singh Berry Kharwanlang is remembered most for his literary achievements. He is generally regarded as having contributed greatly to the perfecting of the written Khasi language, along with Rabon Singh Suka and Jeebon Roy Mairom. Kharwanlang adapted it to the Roman alphabet introduced by British missionaries in the late Nineteenth century. He is also remembered for what is called his "masterpiece," **Ka Jingsneng Tymmen** a compilation of Khasi moral code and rules of etiquette, published in two volumes in 1897, the entire work is written in Khasi, in perfectly rhyming two-line stanzas consisting of ten syllables each. It has 68 stanzas and 374 couplets. At the time of his death he was actively preparing an English-Khasi Dictionary.

Selected Published Works

Ka Jingsneng Tymmen Vol. I, II (Khasi Moral Code).

R.T. RYMBAI

Personal

R.T. Rymbai was born on October 13, 1913 at Jowai in Meghalaya. After completing his education, he assisted in the family business. In 1941, he joined the Assam Civil Service. Later in 1959, he moved to the Indian Administrative Service. He served in various capacities in the districts as Magistrate and in the Assam Civil Secretariat as Under Secretary and Secretary in different departments. After his retirement from the service, he was associated with several commissions and committees, appointed from time to time by Meghalaya State Government, Government of India, the High Court, Guwahati, etc. He was also engaged in social service as President, Shillong College Government Body, President, Seng Khasis College. Beside this he was the President, the Managing Committee Ramakrishna Mission, Shillong. He was the President, Shillong Law College, Life Member, the Indian Red Cross Society, the President, the Seng Khasi and the President, the Sein Jainta.

Education

Rymbai graduated from the Calcutta University in 1937.

Contribution

His contribution in the field of history of Khasis and Jaintia is significant. He also wrote on the social customs, festivals and religion of Pnars (Jaintias) and Khasis. His essays and articles were published in sources of the **Indian History and Khasi Heritage**, etc.

He was president of Khasis Authors Society. He was also convenor of the Meghalaya Chapter of the Indian National Trust for Art & Cultural Heritage from 1985 to 1991. He was Co-ordinator, the Meghalaya Wing of the Indian Classical Music and Cultural Heritage Amongst Youth and Member, Governing Body of the North-East Zone Cultural Centre, Dimapur, as well as Life Member, the North-East India Council for Social Science Research.

Selected Published Works

Ban Pynieng la Ka Rasong (1979), **Ki Riti Ka Ri** (Shaphang ki Rangbah Shnong)(1985).

For Late. Rymbai's Literature please contact—

Madam Lama Hynniwta
Makhane, Jiaw Chappal Road,
Shillon-793002,
Telephone : 0364-2243156

S.S. MAJAW

Personal

S.S. Majaw was born in 1952 in Shillong. His father's name is T.E. Tiengtoh and his mother's name is H.M. Majaw. Presently he is a lecturer in Synod College, Shillong.

Education

He is an M.A.

Contribution

S.S. Majaw is a critic, an essayist and a poet. He writes both in Khasi and English. He has three published books to his credit. At present he is the Treasurer of Khasi Author's Society, Shillong (Meghalaya).

Select Published Works

Ha Ki Sur Ka Poetry, Ke Ese Bad Ai Poem, Ki Syrwet Jingshai.

Contact Information

S.S. Majaw
C/o Madan Ryting
Post : Kam Ryting Shillong
Distt. : Khasi Hills
Shillong (Meghalaya)
Telephone : 0364-2231850

STREAMLET DKHAR

Personal

Born on December 23, 1960, Dkhar is presently a reader in the Khasi Department of North East Hill University, Shillong. She is an active member of several national and regional cultural, educational and literary organisations. She is also a member of the Meghalaya Amateur Boxing Association.

Education

Dr. Dkhar is an M.A. and Ph.D. Her area of specialisation is Khasi drama, and the title of her Ph.D. thesis is **The Concept of Love in Khasi Drama**.

Contribution

Streamlet Dkhar writes poetry, dramas and essays in Khasi and English. Dkhar writes mostly dramas and criticisms on drama. She has also published a collection of her poems and a work on linguistics. A novel titled U Phrarjsngi is in press.

Among other organisations, Dkhar is a Member of BUGS, BPGS in Khasi, the School of Languages, BPGS in Hindi, and the School Board, School of Humanities and Education. She was Vice President of the Khasi Authors' Society (1993-94), Treasurer of the Khasi Authors' Society (1998-99), and Joint Secretary of the Indian Council for Social Welfare (1991 to present). She is also Vice President of All India Poetess Conference and Working President of Khasi Authors' Society, Joint Secratery of Meghalya State Social Welfare Board as well as Secretary of the All India Tribal Litereray Forums' Meghalya Unit.

She has been awared **Mother Teresa Samman-2003** by All India Poetess Conference, Kolhapur.

Selected Published Works

Ka History Bad Jingroi Jingsan Ka (Khasi Drama)—2004, **Ki Ummat Rupa** (poetry)—2003, **Ka Jingbishar Ïa Ka Drama U Baieit Donshkor** (Criticism on Drama)—2003, **U Banlum Bad Ka Baia** (Drama)—2002, **U Raikut** (Drama)—2001, **Na Khriang Ka Dohnud** (Collection of Poems)—2000, **Ka Jinglong Tynrai U Briew Katkum Ki Drama Khasi** (Criticism)—1986, Co-authored, **Ka Mahabharata** (1988) - **Ka Jingbishar la Ka Shangkhawiah Ki Rang** (Criticism)—1998, **Babu H. W. Sten: Ki Jingkynmaw, in Silver Jubilee Souvenir of Syngkhong Kyntiew Ri**—1998. Her atrticles are also published in **Khasi Studies and other souvenirs published from Shillong.**

Contact Information

Stremlet Dkhar
'Casa Pietatis', Golf-Links
Khliehshnong, Shillong-793001
Telephone: 0364-2591296(R) (M) : 09436117479
E-mail: s.dkhar@rediffmail.com

SYLVANUS LAMARE

Personal

Sylvanus Lamare was born in the Jaintia tribe on May 5, 1963. He taught in Bosco Mount under Don Bosco College, Tura from 1988 to 1990. He joined as a guest lecturer in the Khasi Department, North East Hill University (NEHU) in July 1992 and taught there until December, 1997. He got the permanent post of lecturer in St. Edmund's College, Shillong from 1993 and he is still teaching in this college, which is rated as an "A Grade College" by NACC.

Education

Sylvanus Lamare holds a doctorate in Socio-linguistics. Lamare was a gold medalist in M.A. Khasi in 1992. He, had his early schooling at St. Dominic Savio High School Mawkhar, Shillong. Then he went to Sacred Heart Boys' High School, and from then on he had all his education under the care of the Salesians of Don Bosco. He passed his HSLC in 1982 from Meghalaya Board of School Education. He did his pre-university course and degree pass course from St. Anthony's College, Shillong (1982-87) under North East Hill University. He also received his Bachelor of Philosophy from Salesian College Dimapur, in 1988. In the same year he did his honours in English from Dimapur College under NEHU. He completed his Master's in Khasi in 1992, securing the First Class, and was also awarded a Gold Medal. He did his M.Phil. course work in 1994, securing an A Grade, and was allowed to proceed directly to his Ph.D.

Contribution

Lamare is a poet, critic and painter. Lamare's main contribution is in the field of criticism. He has written many articles and research papers on issues related to culture, literature and language. He has also translated several books of the National Book Trust into the Khasi language. His latest book, **Khasi Poetry (1947-2003)**, will be released soon.

He is bent towards research and his contribution is all-round. Many of his former teachers in Don Bosco institution use to call him **jack of all trades.** He has represented Khasi in many national seminars and presented interesting research papers. He has organised many seminars and also acted as a resource person. His website **www.khasilit.org**, which was launched on June 30th, 2002, gives free information through the internet on Khasi literature, language, culture or any other queries on the Khasis. He has answered more than 3000 queries by researchers from all over the world on the different aspects of the Khasis. Lamare wants to share **the riches of Khasi be it language, literature, culture or other aspects with the rest of the world.**

He was in the team of Indian writers which visited China on October 2004 at the invitation of the Chinese Writer's Association. He is also a member of the National Focus Group on the Teaching of Indian Languages, **NCERT** (2004-2005). His motto is, **Let Down Your Nets—Actions Speak Louder Than Words.** His advice to people is **Spend time or else time will spend you.**

Sylvanus Lamare is perhaps the youngest member of the present General Council of the **Sahitya Akademi (2003-2008).**

Selected Published Works

Uei U Dieng (translated into Khasi from *What Is A Tree*)—2001, **Ka Puriskam Ka Jingjynjar** (translated into Khasi from *A Tale Of Troubles*)—2001, **Shisien Ha Nongkyndong** (translated into Khasi from *Once In A Village*)—2001, **U Khun Sing U Nang Ban Kyrhuh** (translated into Khasi from *A Baby Lion Learns To Roar*)—2001, **U Birju Bad U Kulai Uba Her** (translated into Khasi from *Birju and the Flying Horse*)—2001, **H.W. Sten Bad Ka Ktien Khasi**—2000, **Seng Khasi and its Contributions**—1999, **Ki Dak thoh Ktien Jaintia Kamwa Yoo Ha Ka Pnar Grammar Book**—1999, **Khatlai Tylli Ki Parom**—1998, **Ki Tnat Ka Kolshor** (The book is prescribed as a textbook for the 3-year degree as an elective Paper I, since 1993, at the NEHU degree syllabus for Khasi), **Ki Diphthong Ha Ka Pnar Grammar Book**—1999, **Khasi Dance with a Difference, in Meghalaya Gaurdian**—1993, **Tears in Soso Tham's Poems** (A critical study of the poems written by Soso Tham), **Ki Sngi Jong Ngi**, Seminar on the Standardization of Khasi Writing published by SCERT Shillong (Co-authored).

His latest book, released in March, 2004 is entitled **Khasi Poetry** (1947-2003).

Contact Information

Sylvanus Lamare
Casa Pietatis, Golf-links
Khliehshnong, Shillong-793001
Telephone:(R) 0364-2591296
email : sslamare@rediffmail.com

WEBSTER DAVIS JYRWA

Personal

Webster Davis Jyrwa was born in July 6, 1923. He had a long career in All India Radio and was known as a fearless and conscious officer who often risked his life in the discharge of duties. He was the Programme Executive of Kohima Radio Station when it opened in 1963 and in his two years tenure, when the state was in the throes of insurgency, he toured the remotest areas of Nagaland for collection of programmes. In 1983 during the Assam communal riot when all the senior officers had fled from the station, he discharged his duties of incharge of Dibrugarh Station. The credit of setting up the most difficult radio station at Tawang goes to him. This place is covered with snow all the year round and the temperature runs in minus degrees. Jyrwa was incharge of the station from 1973 to 1976. He crossed the SELA Pass, located at an altitude of 15000 ft, more than fifty times in the performance of duties. He was also in the Meghalaya State Service on deputation and served there as the Director, Arts & Culture and Director, the Tribal Institute of Art & Culture. He served as the Vice President of the State Council of Bharat Scouts and Guides, Meghalaya from 1984 till the end of his life and had been fully involved in this noble movement taking part as a scout in all the social and welfare activities. He was also the President, the Meghalaya Society for Community Development, the President, the Langsning Youth Organisation, Chairman, the Press Advisory Committee, Government of Meghalaya.

Contribution

Webster Davis Jyrwa wrote short stories, poetry, essays, dramas, etc., both in Khasi and English. He was also known as an excellent composer of music and script and dialogue writer.

Jyrwa's twelve books of folk stories, fiction, poetry, essays and articles and dramas in Khasi have been published so far. He wrote articles in English too.

He also produced six music cassettes of self-composed songs in Khasi and English. On the occasion of **SAARC** summit in Shillong, he composed a special welcome song in English. He also wrote scripts, dialogues and composed songs and music for the first Khasi tele-film **Ka Nong** and for another tele-film **Tear Drops on the Feather.**

He has also been the leader of the well known JAIAW Orchestra. He led the cultural troupe of the Wangla dance which was performed at the IX Asian Games at Delhi. Another cultural troupe from Meghalaya put up a cultural show in his leadership at Calcutta in 1979.

He was associated with several literary and cultural organizations in various capacities, such as, the President, the Khasi Authors Society, Chairman, the State Advisory Council Arts & Culture, Government of Meghalaya for two terms from 1988 to 1991, the Vice President, the Moral & Cultural Awakening Society, Meghalaya, Adviser, the Meghalaya Artists' Guild for promotion of the art or painting, sculpturing, crafts, etc., Co-convenor, the Meghalaya Chamber of Indian National Trust for Arts & Cultural Heritage, Member, Advisory Committee, the Centre for Creative Arts, North Eastern Hill University, Member, Steering Committee, the Literary and Cultural Studies, N.E.H.U., Executive Member, the North Eastern Zone Cultural Centre, Dimapur, Nagaland, Member, Advisory Committee, the Art & Culture, North East Council, etc.

He is the recipient of six Meghalaya State literary awards and a plaque. He received the **Tirot Sing Memorial Award**-1992, the most prestigious award in the state for his outstanding contribution in the field of art, culture and literature.

Contact Information

Webster Davis Jyrwa
Jaiaw Langsning
Shillong-793002,
(Meghalaya)

Mizoram

Mizo

B. LALTHANGLIANA

Personal

B. Lalthangliana was born on June 16th, 1945 in the village of Khawbung. His father was Ringchina. He is currently a Senior Lecturer in Mizo Language at Hrangbana College in Aizawl.

Education

Lalthangliana was educated in Myanmar and holds Master Degree in History.

Contributions

B. Lalthangliana is a renowned writer in Mizoram. He has also edited a large number of books. Two of his works have been translated—one in English and the other in Barmese. Besides this, he has been doing research works on literature and history. So far, he has written nearly two hundred essays and articles published in various Magazines and Journals.

To date, Lalthangliana has served as President of the Mizo Writers' Association from 2000. He has also served as Secretary, Mizo Academy of Letters (1988-1999), Editor, **Thu leh Hla** (a monthly literary journal) 2000-2001, Chairman, Literature Committee, Hrangbana College, Member, Tribal Art & Culture Adivsory Board, Government of Mizoram, Member, Mizo Language Board, Government of Mizoram, Member, Mizoram Publication Board, Member, Executive Committee INTACH, Mizoram Chapter, Member, Cultural Heritage Committee, Aizawl District, Convener and Architect, Mizo Poets' Square Khawbung, Project Director Study Group, Mizo History & Culture sponsored by NEC, Shillong etc. (1994-2001), and Team Leader, Study Team of Mizo Origin sponsored by Mizoram Government (2000).

Selected Published Works

Zoram Encyclopedia—2003, **Zotawng Bulpui Leh A Hmanna** (Mizo Language and Phrases)—2002, **History & Culture of Mizo in India, Burma & Bangladesh**—2001, **Mi Chungchuang-Rokunga & Zikpuii Pa** (Biographies of Rokunga & Zikpuii Pa)—2000, **Pi Pu Chhuahtlang** (Studies in Mizo Literature)—1998, **History of Mizo Literature** (History of Mizo Literature)—1993, **Hmasang Zonun**—1992 (Cultural History of Mizo), **Mizo Nunhlui-II** (Early Mizo History-II)—1991, **Mizo Nunhlui-I**—1990 (Early Mizo History-I), **Ka Lungkham** (Introducation of Mizo Literature)—1989, **History of Mizo in Burma (English**—1980, **Mizo**—1978, **Burmese**—1975).

Contact Information

B. Lalthangliana
Chhinga Veng, H/No.-A-4,
Aizawl, Mizoram
Telephone : 0389-2322587

C. LAIZAWNA

Personal

C. Laizawna was born on January 10, 1959 in the village of Tualpui, Champhai District Mizoram. His father was Manvela and his mother was Lalduhi.

Education

Laizawna received his education through high school and passed PUC from Champhai College.

Contribution

C. Laizawna is a young Mizo writer. He has been writing articles and books since his college days. He writes short stories, plays and novels, in Mizo. He is also a journalist. He has written more than thirty books, the majority of which are fictional works. He has enriched Mizo literature. The Mizo Academy of Letters declared his book **Hmangaihzuali**, the **Book of the Year** in 1990. This book is now part of the Mizo curriculum in the University. His book **Anita** was declared the **Book of the Year** in 1998 by the Mizo Academy of Letters. Laizawna's many articles have been published in different Magazines. He has also translated a few English books into Mizo. He has translated many children's stories, most of them fairy tales.

Selected Published Works

Novels

A Thlawn Mai Maw (Is it in Vain?)—1999, **Anita** (Novel)—1998, **Ka Thlang Zawk** (She's my choice)—1993, **K.S. Min Ti Maw!?** (You call me a Harlot), **Tah a Tul Leh Thin** (I can't help but cry)—1991, **Ka Fa Asin!** (It's my child)—1991, **Hmangaihzuali** (Hmangaihzuali)—1990, **Mittui Nen** (With tears)—1988, **Chhani** (Chhani)—1987, **Zan Mak Tak** (Marvellous Night)—1986, **Thuruk, Hmangaih Ziri** (Secrecy, pretty Ziri), **Hmaithinghawn** (Impudence without Shame)—1985, **Lei Theihloh Ruali** (Ruali : Priceless Woman)—1985, **Remi Leh Ruata** (Remi and Ruata), **I Ta Ka Ni Si A!** (I belong to you)—1983, **B-2** (B-2)—1982.

Detective Books

Omnus (Omnus)—1994, **I Duh Thlang Rawh** (Choose as You Like)—1991, **Lala Dawhthlak** (Christmas Gift to Lala)—1991, **Christmas Putar** (Santa Claus)—1990, **Duh Luat Vang** (Love Suffers)—1989, **Thih Leh Thih** (Die if you must)—1988, **Sulhnu** (Footprints)—1988, **Inthen Tawh Lo Turin** (Not to part with each other)—1987, **In Hrang** (Haunted House)—1987, **Veh Thlem** (Beguilement)—1987, **Pari Zun** (Pari's Charm)—1987, **Thir Thingrem Thuhruk** (Hidden Box)—1986, **Thani Tan** (For Thani)—1986, **Zalen Hma Chu** (Till we achieve freedom)—1986, **Zungbun Chu** (The Ring)—1986, **A Hlui Thei Lo** (Never Grow Old)—1986.

Books on Drama

Kan Tiam Tawh Si (Since we Vowed)—1982

Books on Moral guidance

Nu Pa Thuruk (Secret of a Couple)—1996, **Chhelna Rah** (Fruit of Patience)—1987, **Engkim Hlawkna** (Productivity)—1986, **Nun Hruaitu** (Moral Guidance)—1985, **Hnehna Thuruk** (A secret of Victory)—1985, **Fa Enkawl Dan** (Child Care)—1984, **Nupa Hlim Nun** (Secret of Married Life)—1983.

Books on Bible-based Stories

Zizyphus—1990, **Nathanael**—1988.

Contact Information

C. Laizawna
Dinthar, Aizawl,
Mizoram, Pin-796001
Telephone: 0389-2326365/2324290 (R)

C. THUAMLUAIA

Personal

Thuamluaia was born in 1922 in the southern part of Mizoram. His father's name was Lalnghinga and mother's name was Darlianchingi. The youngest of five children, he had two brothers and two sisters. Thuamluaia was the Headmaster of the High School of Lunglei until1956. He contested the election of the Assam Assembly in the year 1957, and was elected twice as an MLA. While serving in the Legislature, he established a high school in Saiha in Mizoram. He also become the first Headmaster of that school. He was married to the daughter of Lalzova, the great Mizo songwriter. While still serving actively in politics, on May 29, 1959, Thuamluaia developed a serious headache and died that same day. He was buried in the Lunglei cemetery on May 30, 1959.

Education

Thuamluaia received his Bachelor's Degree from St. Edmund's College, Shillong in 1950.

Contributions

Thuamluaia was a fiction writer and poet. He wrote one novel and three short stories. He also wrote a few poems and literary articles, including three articles in English, which he was unable to publish in his lifetime. These three articles were: **The Disaster, Christian Festivals, The Days That Followed.**

Selected Published Works

Zoram Nipui (Summer in Mizoram), **Kan nun Khuarei an chang tur hi** (How our lives would be fading out), **Tawng hmasawn nan** (For the development of language), **Pu Hmara leilet veng** (The locality of Mr. Hmara).

DARCHHAWNA

Personal

Darchhawna was born on January 26, 1936. He started his career as the headmaster of Thingsai High School in 1960. He then became lecturer at PMG College. Later he served as Principal of Lunglei College, P.U. College and Johnson College. He attended a training course in hockey under Major Dhyanchand in Shillong in 1958. He has also presided over several committees and organizations. He has also visited several countries in the Asia Pacific and South Asia, as well as Italy and France. As a member of the Azad Hind Expedition Team (1995-96) he traced the routes taken by Netaji Subhash Chandra Bose and his army in South East Asia.

Education

Darchhawna holds an M.A. and D.Litt. (Hon.). He holds a Diploma in Music and Adult Education Training. He attended St. Antony's College, the Theological College, Sydney, and the Melbourne College of Divinity, Melbourne. He was also educated in California, USA.

Contribution

Darchhawna has written books on different topics. He has also contributed significantly to the propagation of Hindi in Mizoram. He was president of the Mizoram Hindi Prachar Sabha from 1980 to 2001, and during his tenure he set up 50 Prachar centres, eight schools and one Rashtrabhasha Mahavidyalaya. He has written several articles and leaflets in magazines which encourage the use of Hindi. He received the Presidential Award in 1999 for his work on Hindi language propagation. Darchhawna delivered lectures in different countries of South East Asia during the Azad Hind Expedition, 1995-96. He has been a regular contributor to All India Radio and Doordarshan since 1963.

Darchhawna has also submitted and delivered a number of papers for national and state-level seminars in both English and Mizo.

Darchhawna is deeply interested in music, literature, art, theology and culture. Darchhawna has served as a member of the General Council of the Sahitya Akademi (1991-96), Sangeet Natak Akademi (1990-1992), the Hindi Salahakar Samiti (GOI 2001-2003), the Hindi Literature Selection Board (2001-2002), Fellow of the United Writers Association, and the Lalit Kala Akademi (1992-1994).

He was given the Bharat Ratna Award in 2001 and Bharat Jyoti Award in 1999. He has also been Awarded by Mizo Sahitya Academy. He got Padma Shri Award in 2005.

Selected Published Works

Music Dictionary—2004, **Savidge Leh Lorrain-Te Mizo Literature-ah an Hnathawh** (Contributions of Savidge and Lorrain on Mizo Literature)—2004, **Hla Siamtu Hmingthangte** (A Gallery of Great Musicians)—2003, **Khawvel History& Culture** (World History and Culture)—2002, **Upate Rawngbawlna** (Senior Citizens and their Participation in Society)—2002, **Kohhran Chanchin** (Church History)—1999, **Beisei Ram** (My Literary Works)—1999, **Kum Sang Rorel** (Millennial Kingdom)—1998, **Kohhran Thurain** (Doctrine of The Church)—1998, **Mizo Culture**, (Mizo Culture)—1993, **Khawthlang Music & Mizo Culture** (Western Music and Mizo Culture)—1992, **Music Theory** (Music Theory)—1984, **Baptist Inkaihhruaina** (Baptist Principles)—1976, **Naupang Zirlaibu** (Junior Lessons)—1975, **Zirtirtu** (Teacher)—1974, **Thim ata Engah** (From Darkness to Light)—1974, **Music Zirna** (Rudiments of Music)—1970.

Contact Information

Darchhawna
Kulikawn, Aizawl
Mizoram-796005
Telephone : 0389-2323570 (R)

DENGCHHUANA

Personal

Dengchhuana was born on April 7, 1929 in the Kulikawn locality of Aizawl (Mizoram). He died on May 11, 2004. His father's name was Lalhlira and his mother's name was Mitinchhingi. He had nine brothers and sisters. In 1968 he took the Assam Civil Service Examination, where he secured fifth position. He then joined the Civil Service and worked in different parts of Assam.

Education

Dengchhuana pursued his education in Shillong since there was no high school in Mizoram when he was a student. Dengchhuana was just eleven years old when he joined high school. However, due to family problems he could not continue his education as a regular student and he completed his matriculation as a private student. He could not attend classes as a regular student for his Intermediate and Bachelor's Degrees as well, and studied as a private student up to his Master's Degree.

Contibutions

Delghhuana wrote ten books, mostly essays on literature. His last book, named *Hringchan Piallei*, consisted of Thirtyone articles over more than 200 pages. In addition to writing, he was very interested in translation work. He translated books of Omar Khayam into the Mizo language. He also translated Ravindra Nath Tagore's *Gitanjali* into Mizo. He also translated some Mizo folksongs into English, such as the following one—

Let me be a flower, indeed a/wild flower
Growing by the path oft' trod/by my love
May she pluck me at least / for child's delights

He was loved by other intellectuals for his witty sayings and writings. At the time of his death, Dr. Laltluangliana Khiangte, a renowned writer, poet, playwright and research scholar, expressed great sorrow on behalf of the writers' community:—

Who am I to weep for you ?
Tears of sadness flow like a summer spring,
The sudden demise at this odd hour,
Reminds how great thy soul for us all,
Shanti, Shanti, on Earth you rest in peace,
Till we meet again in our Heavenly home. Amen.

Selected Published Works

Sangzuala Pa Kutchhuak (Literary Works of Delghhuana), **Hringchan Piallei** (Collection of Essays), **Duhaisam** (Ideals), **Duhaisam-ii** (Volume of Ideals), **Bible A Thu Inthup Leh Scientist-te** (Secret Code of The Bible and Scientist), **Pathian Tihdamna Leh Doctor Te Thiamna** (Divine Healing & Medical Science).

Contact Information

Dengchhuana
C/o Mrs. Vanrami
Tuikhuahtlang
Aizawl-796001(Mizoram)

JAMES DOKHUMA

Personal

James Dokhuma was born on June 15, 1932 in Sialsuk in a peasant family. His father's name was Scrangchechina and mother's name was Katkungi. He taught Hindi in a high school during his service career, but now, after retirement, he devotes his time to writing. He is also active in politics and has a reputation as a good orator.

Education

Educated up to 5th class, James also completed a military certificate course.

Contributions

James Dokhuma is a Mizo poet, short story writer, dramatist, essayist, historian and journalist. He has written over thirty books. He has written in all genres including poetry, short stories, dramas, novels, autobiographies, histories, essays and travelogues.

He has been honoured with various awards such as the **Bhasha Samman**, **Padmashri**, and the **Academy Award**. He also got **Mizo Acedemy Awards** for Best Writers of the year 5 times for the years 1984,1886,1988,1991,1996.

Selected Published Works

Singapore—a Mizo Saltangte—2002 (War Prisoners in Singapore), **Lamsuaka** (Fate of Lamsuaka)—2001, **Ch. Chhunga Chanchin**—1999 (Biography of Ch. Chhunga), **Thla Hleinga Zan (Vol.II)**—1999 (Full Moon-II), **Zokhaw Nun**—1998 (Village Life), **Ka Thinlung Luangliam**—1996 (My Poems), **Rilru far Chhuak**—1995 (Collection of Essays), **Mak & Mak**—1995 (Pyramid), **An Va Hlu En Thilnung Tinreng**—1995 (How Precious They Are!), **Netaji Subhas Chandra Bose**—1993 (Netaji Subhas Chandra Bose), **Hmeichhia Leh Mipa Indona**—1993 (War Between Men & Women),

Hmanlai Mizo Kalphung—1992 (Mizo History), **Silaimu Ngaihawm**—1992, **Khawhar In**—1990 (House of Mourning), **Chhungkua Sipai Inkhawm Thupui**—1990 (Home), **Lonesome Cowboy**-1990, **Ka Hlahril** (My Poems)—1989, **Tawng Un Hrilhfiahna**—1989 **(Difficult Words & Their Meaning)**, **Gabbatha**—1989 (Gabbatha), **Nunna Bu-a Hmimg Chuangte**—1986 (Book of Life), **Kimoto, Syonora**—1984 (Good Bye, Kimoto), **Good bye, Lushai Brigade**—1983 (Good bye, Lushai Brigade), **Notes on idioms & Phrases for H/s**—1983, **Hmangaihna Thuchah**—1982 (Message of Love), **Irrawady Lui Kamah**—1982 (On the Bank of Irrawady), **Rinawmin**—1981 (Yours Sincerely), **Tumpangchal Nge Saithangpuii**—1981(Wild Gayal and Saithangpuii), **Ka Inpuanna**-1981 (My Confession), **Finna Hmahruai**—1980 (Wisdom), **Arsi Thawnthu**—1979 (Story of Stars), **Hausak Aiin Hrisel a Hlu Zawk**—1978 (Health is better than wealth), **Ni Leh Thla Karah Leng**—1978 (Sailo Clan), **Hmasawnna**—1978 (Development), **Thla Hleinga Zan**—1977 (Full Moon), **Khawtlang Inzirna**—1977 (Public instruction), **Tumna Chu a hlawhling Thin**—1976 (Will Succeed), **Zoram Tualto Kohhran Chanchin**—1975 (Religious sects originated in Mizoram).

Contact Information

James Dokhuma
Kulikawn, Aizawl-796001
Mizoram
Telephone: 0389-2323390

J. MALSAWMA

Personal

J. Malsawma was born on February 28, 1930 at Lungsum village, 63 miles north of Aizawl in Mizoram. His father's name was Lianhnawka. He took active part in scouting and became a King's Scout (now President's Scout) with 24 proficiency badges. He also became a Cubmaster and Assistant Scoutmaster. He was enrolled as an Advocate of the Assam High Court in 1985, and practiced law for five years. Malsawma joined the Mizoram Civil Service in 1962 and served there in various capacities, such as Magistrate & Revenue officer, Under Secretary to Government of Mizoram, Law and Judicial Dept., Deputy Secretary to Government of Mizoram, Secretariat Administration, General Administration and D.P.& A.R., Secretary & Director, Local Administration Department, Secretary Mizoram Legislative Assembly, and Director, Administrative Training Institute. He retired from service in 1988 and was thereafter re-employed for one year. He took keen interest in social work and associated himself with various organizations. Some of his roles inlude:

President, T.Z.Y.M.A, (1946-48), President, Central Young Mizo Association (1964-65), Adviser, Mizoram Vigilance Council, Executive Member, Mizoram Guardian, President, Mizo Students' Association, Part-time Lecturer, Pachhunga Memorial College, Aizawl, Member, Committee of Mizo Customary Law.

Education

M.A. and LL.B.

Contributions

Malsawma has written more than one hundred articles and essays on various topics and published five books. These books were written mainly for students who have undertaken Mizo as their degree subject and in post-graduate courses.

His book entitled **Zozia** contains the ethics and moral philosophy of the Mizo, their cultures and traditions, social values etc. The first edition was so popular that it sold out within a few months. It was reprinted and the second edition has also sold out now.

He wrote a book, **Vanglai** that contains biographical information on the author, selected of the author's best essays, information about old Mizo religion and philosophy, and also the biographies of a few prominent Mizo citizens.

His book **Mizo Poems : Old and New** (1962) created a furor. It contains various types of Mizo poems, most of which were handed down orally before Mizoram came under British rule. These poems were almost forgotten and the Church leaders branded them as anti-Christian.

He is also a member of the State Advisory Board on Tribal Art, Culture and Language and Indian National Trust for Arts & Cultural Heritage. He was associated with Mizo Academy of Letters as its Founder-Secretary (1964-65) and later its Adviser. He is presently Member of the Mizoram Publication Board.

In appreciation of his works, the **Mizo Academy of Letters awarded** its highest award, the Academy Award, to Malsawma in November 2001. The Mizo Writer's Association has also awarded to Malsawma the Certificate of Appreciation as many as three times in recongnition of his works.

Selected Published Works

Zozia (Ethics & Moral Philosophy of the Mizo People)—2003, **Vanglai** (Prime Days)—1995, **Notes on Mizo Poems**—1969, **Zonun** (Collection of Essays on Mizo Culture)—1963, **Mizo Poems-Old & New**—1962.

Contact Information

J. Malsawma
B/37, Macdonald Hill, Zarkawt, Aizawl,
Mizoram, Pin : 796001
Telephone: 0389-2341000

KHAWLKUNGI

Personal

Khawlkungi was born on September 14, 1927 in Mission Vengthlang in Aizawl, Mizoram. She is a retired government servant. Khawlkungi has received many awards for her diverse activities. She also received a **war medal** during the Second World War for her work as equipment assistant in the Women Auxiliary Corps (India) in the Air Force Unit at Calcutta.

Education

Her educational qualification is class -VIII.

Contribution

She is a novelist, story writer, dramatist, essayist, journalist, and editor. She has also written an autobiography and has worked as the editor of **Runlum** Magazine, published by M.H.I.P. Khawlkungi writes mainly fiction. She writes in Mizo with the Roman script. Her first book, the one that also started her career, was **Sangi Rinawmna**. She has many books to her credit, for which she has received several awards. She has contributed around thirty-two plays and stories, four prose books, ten biographies, and many poetry and stories, translated from English into Mizo.

In 1977 she received First Prize in the **Zawlpala Thlan Tlang**, play and story writing competition. This work was also selected to be a text in the B.A. course as a major subject. She again received a first prize for her story named **Monusal** in 1983. She received the **Padma Shri Award** in 1987 for her contribution to Mizo literature. In 1988 she received the Special Service Star for the Girl Guides while she was working as Assistant State Commissioner. Khawlkungi received an **Academy Award** from the Academy of Letters of Mizoram in 1998.

Selected Published Works

Chantawka Khawrel (Fate)—2003, **Thawnthu-7** (7-Stories)—2001, **Lemchan Thawnthu Thlan Chhuah** (Selected Plays)—1998, **Thawnthu 70** (70 Stories)—1998, **Duhtak Sangpuii** (Dearest Sangpuii)—1998, **Kan Chhehvel Ram Thawnthu** (Stories of our Neighbour States)—1992, **Hmanlai Mi thianghlimte** (Saints of olden Days)—1990, **Thawnthu Za** (100 Stories)—1989, **Thawnthu 8** (8 Stories)—1989, **Thawnthu- 7** (7 Stories)—1988, **Hmanlai Hian Maw** (Once Upon a time)—1987, **Girl Guide Thawnthu** (History of Girl Guide)—1984, **Zawlpala Thlan Tlang** (Graveyard of Zalwpala)—1983, **Thawnthu Tawi** (Short Stories)—1983, **Pasal Duhthlan** (Choice of a Husband)—1982, **Thawnthu 5** (5 Stories)—1982, **Thawnthu 3** (3 Stories)—1981, **Lal Fapa Leh Kutdawh** (Prince and the Beggar)—1981, **Moody—A Chanchin Tawi** (Life History of Moody)—1980, **Krista Thih Ni** (The day Christ Died)—1980, **Fahrah Nun** (Orphan's Life)—1979, **Thawnthu Min Hrilh Rawh** (Tell me the story)—1979, **A Tlai Lutuk Ta** (Its too Late)—1979, **Thawnthu- 2** (2-Stories)—1978, **Sangi Rinawmna** (Honesty of Lady Sangi)—1978, **Monu Sual** (Wicked Bride).

Contact Information

Khawlkungi
M-52, Mission Vengthlang,
Aizawl
Mizoram, Pin : 796005

LALTLUANGLIANA KHIANGTE

Personal

L.T. Liana Khiangte was born on June 28, 1961 in Saitual, in the Aizawl District in Mizoram. His parents were T. H. Thanga and Darngeni. Khiangte is an academician and scholar, a Reader (& Head), in the Mizo Department of Mizoram University. His bio-data was included in the *Distinguished Leadership Directory* of 1997 by the ABI, USA and Asia **Pacific Who's Who** of 2000.

Education

L.T. Liana Khiangte is an MA in English with Linguistics. He received a Ph.D. in English-Mizo literature from North-East Hill University in 1991. He pursued his post-doctoral research in folklore and modern Mizo literature and was awarded a Doctorate of Literature in 1999.

Contribution

L.T. Liana Khiangte is an eminent Mizo playwright, essayist, poet, folklorist and scholar-critic. Khiangte started writing when he was a student in the tenth standard in 1977. He has written many works and published twenty eight books in Mizo and in English. He has written more than Thirty plays in Mizo, Sevanteen of which have been published in book form. He has also presented over Hundred papers in national, regional and state-level seminars and conferences. He has also written and contributed over Sixty hundred articles in various journals and periodicals.

His Bio-data was included in the National Sahitya Akademi's **Who's Who of Indian Writers**-1999. He is an academic counsellor for the Master's degree in English under IGNOU and a member of the Mizo Language Board and Mizoram Publication Board for the Government of Mizoram. He is the present Chairman of Board of Studies-Mizo(for both Post Graduate & Under-graduate), Mizoram University; Member-BUGS, NEHU; President of ZOPPEN (Mizo

Poet-Playwright-Essayist-Novelist Club, International) and Member of the Sahitya Akademi General Council (National Academy of Letters 2003-2007), Member of Sangeet Natak Akademi 2004-2008 (National Academy of Music, Dance & Drama), Vice-President of All India Tribal Literary Forum, President of AITLF Eastern North-East zone, Vice-President of ASSITEJ-India (Theatre Group), President of MASLET-India (Multi-purpose Academy), and President of Young Mizo Association (active social organisation) in his locality at Aizawl. He is convenor of North-East rigional committee of all India Tribal Literary Forum and also a member of its central committee at the National level.

Khiangte has been awarded many prizes and awards such as: Book of the Year Award-1997, Best Writer Award-thrice in 2002 and 2003 and 2004, (Most outstanding litterateur in the state), Distinguished Playwright Award-2002, Rastriya Lok Bhasha Samman-2003 (National Award).

Selected Published Works

In English

World Literature—2005, **The Golden Lines**—2004, **Memorable Poems ans Essays—2003**, **Mizo Songs and Folk Tales** (Sahitya Akademi)—2001, **An Introduction to Mizo Literature** (Papers and Poems)—2001, **Spirit of Night** (Collection of Poems and Papers)—2001, **Folklore-1 : Folktales of Mizoram**—1997, **Mizo Drama: Origin, Development & Themes** (Cosmo Publications, New Delhi)—1993, and several educational help books for students of literatures and language.

In Mizo

Lunghlu (Diamond)—2004, **Zalenpar** (Blooming of Free Thought : Collection of Literary essays)—2003, **Thlaler Nula** (Forlorn Lady)—2002, **Hamlet leh a Ziaktu**—2002, **Thlifim** (Collection of Mizo Poetry)—2001, **Chantual Ennawm (Collection of short plays)**—2001, **Liangkhaia Lungphun** (Great author and his works)—2000, **Mizo Thuziak Thlan Chhuahte** (Prose writings)—1999, **Mizo Hlahril Thlan Chhuahte** (Mizo songs and poems)—1999, **Infiamna**

Khawvel Leh Rawngbawina—1998, **Pasaltha Khuangchera** (Historical Play)—1997, **Biakliana Robawm** (Writer and his works)—1996, **Thuhlaril** (Trends and History of Mizo Literature)—1995, **Lemchan Khawvel-I: Lalnu Ropuiliani** (Collection of three Mizo Historial Dramas)—1994, **Thalai Chanchin** (History of Christian youth movement in Mizoram)—1993, **Chanchintha Meichher** (Gospel Centenary drama)—1993, **Lehkhabu Ramtiam** (Collection of Literary Essays)—1993, **Thupui Zirbingte** (Literary Workshop papers)—1989, **Thupui Pawimawh Pali** (Four important themes)—1989.

Contact Information

Dr. L.T. Liana Khiangte
Reader & Head,
Mizo Department
Mizoram University, Aizawl
Telephone: 0389-2348143, Fax: 0389-2340313 / 2348143

Residence

B-43, Fakrun, Mission Veng, Aizawl
Mizoram, India—796001
Telephone : 0389-2326365 / 232550
Mobile : 9436141119 (Aizawl), 9891326766 (Delhi)
E-mail: drltkhiangte@yahoo.co.in & ltlkhiangte@hotmail.com

LALSANGZUALI SAILO

Personal

Lalsangzuali Sailo was born on May 15, 1949 to Vanchhuma Sailo and Sapthangi Chawngthu in Thingsai, Mizoram. At present she is the Headmistress of Government JL Higher Secondary School in Aizawl. She is married to Laldinliana and has two sons and one daughter.

She is also famous for her luxuriant two metre long hair, which she has claimed is the longest in the world. **Gulf Daily News**, Bahrain, also published a feature on her in April 1986. **The Sunday Magazine** also praised her hair in **Locks, Her Key to Fame.**

Sailo is deeply interested in Mizo weaving, embroidery and knitting. She has produced Sixty pieces of home-spun clothing. She is the teacher-in-charge of work experience in her school.

Sailo has been the Branch President of the **Mizo Hmeichhia Insuihkhawn Pawl** (All Mizo Women Organisation) since 1984, and was an Executive Committee member from 1984 to 1989 in the MHIP Headquarters.

Education

Sailo matriculated in 1968 from St John Bosco's Convent. She received her B.A. (with Honours) from St Mary College, Shillong. After completing her B.Ed she became a teacher. She received her Ph.D. in **Mizo Literature**. After it she got D.Litt. on **folk literature and modern Mizo literature**.

Contribution

Sailo's songs, essays and stories have been published in various magazines and newspapers. She has authored Sevanteen books and three booklets. Her favourite work is **Tlawm Ve Lo Lalnu Ropuiliani,** the story of a Mizo freedom fighter. **Thuthulung Thar Hmeichhiate** (Women of the New Testament) and **Sakhming Chul Lo** (Names That Will Not Fade or Be Forgotten) examines the history of the

Mizo poetess **Khuangthli.** She has also examined issues involving the preservation of wildlife and the environment in her work.

In addition to her excellence in literature, she is a well-known soloist and music composer. She has performed on the radio and TV as a soloist and has twenty six albums to her credit. This is the highest number of song albums released by a Mizo singer. Her performances have taken her to hundreds of cities in India, as well as to the United States and Canada. Sailo has composed over three hundred sixty songs of which seven are in English. She was honoured as Best Composer in Mizo for several years.

She is an eminent Mizo writer and is also well-known as a singer and music composer. She received the **Padma Shri Award** for her contributions. Associated with nearly 20 organisations in Mizoram, she is actively engaged in social, cultural and literary activities.

Sailo's name was included in the **Who's Who column of Current Topics** in January 1977. Lorry Lutz, editor of **Power Magazine** in California, wrote a booklet about Sailo entitled **Her Grandpa was a Head Hunter.**

L. Sailo got many prizes and awards at State and National levels for literature, social work and music, some of them are mentioned below.

Woman of the Year, 1975 in the first popularity poll organized by Aizawl College, Aizawl, **First Prize** in **Pick Your Pop** 1981, 1982 and 1983 as the best song composer organized by Ainawn Teenage Weekly, **Most Outstanding Woman Litterateur of the Decade in Mizoram** organized by Lelte Weekly in 1984, **The Best Song Composer Award** in the year 1984, 1988, 1991, 1992 and 1996, **Most Outstanding Litterateur,** 1994 organised by Lelte Weekly; **Writer of the Year 1998** by Mizo Writers Association, **All India Radio Outstanding Artiste**–1998, **The Greatest Singer of the Century** by Zolentu Magazine in 2000, **Pu Buanga Award** 2000 by Mizo Academy of Letters Jt Headquarters, Lunglei for her contribution to Mizo literature, **Padma Shri Award** in 1998, Several **certificates** of honour from various organizations for her contribution in the fields of education and social welfare.

Selected Published Works

Ka Hring Lamtluang (Autobiography)—2003, **Tlawm ve lo Lalnu Ropuiliani** (History of the Great Mizo Chieftainess)—1999-2000, **Ka Inpuanna** (My Experiences)—1999-2000, **Khuangthli** (Biscofia Javanica) (a book on environment and wildlife)—1999, **Kulva** (The Drongos) (a book on environment and wildlife)—1998, **Sakhming Chul Lo** (History of Mizo Women Song Composers)—1995, **Devotional Songs & Songs for Children** (with Tonic Solfa)—1991, **Children's Song Book**—1990, **Lunglen Hnem** (Comforting the Loneliness)—1987, **Songs composed by Lalsangzuali Sailo**, Vols. I and II—1984, **Famngai Hnemtu** (Songs)—1984, **Songs/Hymns composed by Lalsangzuali Sailo** (with Tonic Solfa)—1977.

Contact Information

Lalsangzuali Sailo
C/9, Nurseryveng, Aizawl,
Mizoram-796001
Telephone: 0389-2335905/
Mo.-09436141560

L. BIAKLIANA

Personal

L. Biakliana was born in Mission Veng Aizawl on August 26, 1918. His father, Reverend Liangkhaia, was a Preacher and Pastor and his mother, Ngurchhuani, was the daughter of the chief of Saitual Village, now in Aizawl District of Mizoram.

At the age of Eighteen, when he wanted to be graduated, Biakliana was infected with tuberculosis, which was then an incurable disease. He was hospitalised at Durtlang Hospital, confined and segregated in an isolated building called the **Inte Thawveng**, which means **Small Airy Hut**. His friend Kaphleia, who was also infected with the same disease, was confined in the same building.

After he was discharged from the hospital and his health had improved, he devoted himself to various programmes for social development of his village. He started local chapters of the Boy Scouts, Girl Guides, Bull Bulls, Wolf Cubs and a Church Choir. He also founded a society named **L.Ch.P**, which means, **learners society for reading** in the Mizo language.

Biakliana was struck with tuberculosis again and he ultimately succumbed to the disease at Robert Hospital, Shillong, Meghalaya on October 17th, 1941. His mortal body was laid to rest by his father at a burial ground in Jaiaw, Shillong.

Education

Biakliana remained an undergraduate due to his extended illness.

Contribution

L. Biakliana is considered to be the first Mizo novelist. While in the hospital along with his friend Kaphleia, the two composed poems and novels and translated English poems into Mizo. They even published a hand-written Mizo newspaper called **Chhura Newspaper**. He also reproduced stories and folklore which he read in the books of

John Ruskin, H.G. Adams, R.L. Stevenson, Thackeray, Agatha Christie, Mary Corelli and H.R. Haggard. This storytelling spread the seeds for an awakening to literature by the villagers and broadened their knowledge. Later, on the advice of Reverend Mendus and his father Reverend Liangkhaia, he began to study theology and eventually attended Cherra Theological College, Meghalaya.

Biakliana's novels and poems have only recently become well-known. H. Lalrinfela (Mafaa) now considers him to be **the father of Mizo Poetry.** Laltluangliana Khiangte, an eminent writer and critic of Mizo literature, refers to Biakliana as **the first Mizo novelist.** Biakliana wrote popular novels and several poems. In 1936, at the young age of 18, he wrote the novel **Hawilopari** and in 1937 he wrote the short story **Lali.** These two works have been included in the vernacular textbooks of Mizoram schools and colleges because of their great literary value.

Selected Published Works

Lali (the first Mizo short story)—1937, **Hawilopari** (the first Mizo Novel)—1936 .

Contact Informations

L. Biakliana
C/o Dr. L.T. Liana Khiangte
B-43, Mission Veng
Aizawl-796001
(Mizoram)

LALHMINGLIANA SAIAWI

Personal

Lalhmingliana Saiawi was born on July 1, 1940 in the village of Kawlkulh in Mizoram. His father's name is Thlahaia and mother's name is Lalruni. His mother made him go to school in February, 1945, by giving him a stern order from her sickbed. She did not recover from her illness and she died without knowing that her son became the brightest pupil of Kawlkulh Primary School. He joined government service as an IAS officer on July 18, 1964 and served in the Maharashtra cadre until he took voluntary retirement to join the Maharashtra Administrative Tribunal (MAT), Bombay, as a member on April 1st, 1993. He served as a member of the MAT until March 31, 1998. Again he served as a member of the Central Administrative Tribunal (CAT), Patna Bench from April, 1999 until the end of December, 2001. One important reason for taking voluntary retirement from the IAS was that he would be in a better mood and position to write. He wrote nine books after he took voluntary retirement. Now he is a pensioner, drawing three small pensions.

Education

B.A. (Hons) in Economics.

Contributions

Saiawi has written more than one hundred articles in Mizo on various cultural, social, political, and religious topics which have been published in several magazines and daily newspapers. His articles are always written with a touch of humour. His first article was published in March, 1957, in an Aizawl weekly, **Zoram Thupuan.** Two articles in English were published in a Bombay tabloid, **The Daily,** in 1994. Now he writes articles in Mizo dailies as well as monthly magazines. He also writes occasional humour articles in **Harmony**, which is the monthly newsletter of the IAS officers' Association of Maharashtra.

Many of his English/Mizo articles are occasionally broadcast on All India Radio.

He has written ten books in Mizo, of which six are novels. He is now working on another novel which he is planning to publish soon. He is also planning to publish the second volume of his autobiography, as well as another novel.

His fifth novel, **Keimah Unionliana,** was the first to be printed in Mizoram. But this edition had many misprints as well as some small omissions. Originally, he intended to write the novel in English but later he decided to write it first in Mizo and then translate it into English. Now instead of translating it, he is planning to rewrite the book or some of its parts.

His writings are well-received and appreciated by many readers.

Selected Published Works

A Na Lua (It's Painful)—2002, **Kan Ram Lamah-II** (A Collection of Articles-II) —1999, **Nukawki Fanu** (Nukawki's Daughter)—1998, **Ka Lo Tawn Ve-I** (Autobiography)—1997, **Keimah Union Liana** (Me A Union Liana)—1997, **Nukawki** (Life of Nukawki)—1996, **Lungrang Hmangaihna** (Lungrang Love)—1995, **Lungrang Laiawrha** (Laiawrha of Lungrang Village)—1993, **Thukhaw Chang-I** (A collection of Articles)—1989, **Thukhaw Chang**-III (A collection of Articles-I).

Contact Information

Lalhmingliana Saiawi
Chltlang
P.O. : Aizawl
Pin : 796012 (Mizoram)

REV. LIANGKHAIA

Personal

Rev. Liangkhaia was born in late 1884. He was an eminent Mizo pastor, theologian, evangelist, preacher, historian, folklorist, poet, native astronomer, and musician, as well as a prolific writer. His father happened to be a traditional Mizo knight named Thanghluta, who had achieved great fame by beheading his enemy when he was the chief of his village, Vanpuilala, and plundered the adjoining plain, where non-Mizos lived. Liangkhaia was also one of the most popular personalities among the Mizo people even during his own lifetime. He died on June 27, 1979.

Education

Rev. Liangkhaia managed to learn reading and writing all by himself in a remote village where there was no teacher. Using the inner white side of a stick of bamboo as a sheet of paper, he used to write with a piece of charcoal. In spite of these hardships, he topped the lower primary examination in the town of Aizawl in the year 1908. He pursued further education in the Theological School of Cherrapunji (now Sohra in Meghalaya). There he earned three different certificates of honor in the language, Tonic Solfa, up to intermediate.

Contributions

Rev. Liangkhaia is considered to be the **most established writer amongst the Mizos of the first educated generation**. He was a great Mizo writer He also became the **first Mizo historian** in 1926. He wrote some books on history, culture (including traditional religious practices), theology and language. He composed more than twenty songs and poems. He has also translated over 20 devotional songs from English to the Mizo language. He was one of the foremost Mizo writers, contributing to many different monthly journals from 1911 until his death.

Appreciating all his endeavours, works and contributions, the Mizo Academy of Letters (the leading Mizo literary organisation) awarded him their **most prestigious State Literary Award, the Academy Award**, in 1979. Since then, this literary organisation has continued to give this award to other deserving writers.

Selected Published Works

On History

Kohhran siamthatna bul (Reforming the Churches)—1967, **Thuthlung hlui leh Thuthlung thar kar thu** (About the Old and New Testament)—1954, **Kohhran hrang hrang chanchin** (History of different churches)—1950, **Mizo Chanchin-Part I & II** (History of Mizo, Part I & II)—1938 &1947.

On Culture

Mizo mi leh thil hmingthangte leh Mizo sakhua (Some popular Mizo religions)—1977, **Mizoram Harhna** (Revival in Mizoram)—1972, **Mizo Awmdan Hlui** (Old traditions of Mizos)—1970, **Zoram luh hma Pawi rama la awm lai leh Zoram luh tirh Mizo hla hlui lawrkhawm** (Collection of traditional songs)—1926.

On Theology

Bible Pathian Thu (Bible—God's Words)—1976, **Pathian chatuan remruat** (God's Eternal Plan)—1974, **Pathian Thu Tluantling** (The Fullness of the Gospel)—1972, **Hebrai mite lehkhathawn hrilhfiahna** (Commentary on the book of Hebrew)—1962, **Kohhran leh a rawngbawl hna** (The Church & its Ministry)—1957, **Rom hrilhfiahna** (Commentary on the books of Rome)—1956, **Chhandamna Thu** (About Salvation)—1952, **Thusawm pek hrilhfiahna** (Ten Commandments)—1949, **Thupuan hrilhfiahna** (Commentary on The Revelation)—1941, **Timothea hrilhfiahna** (Commentary on the letter to Timothy), **Ephesi mite lehkhathawn hrilhfiahna** (Commentary on the the book of Ephesi), **Galatia mite lehkhathawn hrilhfiahna** (Commentary on the book of Galatia), **Petera Lehkhathawn Hrilhfiahna** (Commentary on Peter's letter).

On Astronomy

Arsi Chanchin (Mizo concept of the stars)—1975.

Translation from English to Mizo

Indona Thianghlim (The Holy War)—1971, **Bible Dictionary**—1971 **Kristiante Thurin** (Marcus Wards-I)—1970, **Kristiant Thurin** (Marcus Wards-II)—1970, **Sakhaw Khaikhinna** (Comparison of Religions)—1941.

Contact Information

Rev. Liangkhaia
C/o Dr. L.T. Khiangte
B-43, Fakrun Mission Veng
Aizawl-796001, Mizoram
Telephone : 0389-2326365, 2325220

LALENGMAWIA RALTE

Personal

Lalengmawia Ralte was born on October 14, 1947. His father was Lalliana. He is married to Lalrokimiand, has four children, and works as a teacher in a primary school in Venghlui. He has also served as the Registrar of Births and Deaths.

Mr. Ralte is a social worker, mostly concerned with social reforms, a topic on which he has written several papers. He has also held the positions of the Secretary of Village Adult Education, the Member of Mizoram Publication Board, Subject Expert Committee, MBSE, and Secretary, Young Mizo Association.

Contributions

Lalengmawia Ralte has written many books on various subjects like social custom, culture, nature, relegions, drugs and social and human values in various genre. His comittment to social work reflexes in his writings also.

Selected Published Works

Inneihna (Marriage)—2002, **Rahbi Inthup** (Hidden Step)—2000, **Tuihna Thianghlim** (Clear Water-spring)—2000, **A Tlo Lo** (Not Lasting)—1999, **Happy Home**—1999, **Chhum Zinna Ram** (Land covered with clouds)—1995, **Aigupta Sabel** (Egyptian Wealth)—1992, **Krismas Drama** (Christmas Drama)—1990, **Khawngaihna Batu** (A Debtor of Grace)—1990, **A Va Pawi Em !** (It's A Pty!)—1989, **Ka Nu, Min Hrilh Rawh** (Mom, Tell it to Me)—1989, **Ka Thianghlim Tawhlo** (I' m No Longer a Virgin)—1989, **Eternal Bliss** (Eternal Bliss)—1988, **Never Leave Me Alone** (Never Leave me Alone)—1987, **Min Thungrul Suh** (Don't Repay Me)—1987, **Tu Fa Nge?** (Whose Child is it?)—1968, **Honeymoon** (Honeymoon)—1985, **Khawdur Kara Chhimbal** (Blessing in Disguise)—1984, **Drugs Hlau Rawh** (Beware of Drugs)—1983, **Kan Hlimna Tur** (For our happiness)—1983, **Eng vang nge?** (Why?)—1983, **A Sawt Tawh Lo** (Too Late)—1981, **Beidawn Mai Lovah Aw !** (No Desperation), **I Tana Tawk** (Enough for You)—1986.

Contact Information

Lalengmawia Ralte
Venghlui Vill.,
P.O. : Aizawl-796001,
Mizoram
Telephone : 0389-2326610

LALHMUAKA

Personal

Lalhmuaka was born in 1912. He is married to Laltawani and has four children. He also taught in Government High School, Shillong (1937), Government Boy's School Middle School (1940), Government High School, Aizawl (1944-1957). He was the Headmaster, Government High School, Lunglei from 1957-1969. He retired as the Headmaster of the same school.

Education

He is a B.A. from NEHU, Shillong.

Contributions

Lalhuaka has written numerous articles and seminar papers. He has given talks on All India Radio (AIR) and Doordarshan (DD).

He has traced the History of Mizo and also conducted research on the persecution of early Mizo Christians. He has also written a biography of a famous woman Mizo dancer during World War I (1914-1918) named **Hrang Chhawni**. It was published in 2003. He has also written textbooks especially for Arithmetic and Mathmatics students of class eight to ten.

Selected Published Works

Lal Isua Tuahrem Mizoram (Mizoram—Handiworr of Christ)—2002, **Hrangchhawni** (Biography of Hrangchhawani)—1994, **Zoram History-1800-1950** (History of Mizoram From 1800-1950)—1992, **Zoram Sikul Zirna Chanchin** (Learning in Mizoram Schools)—1992, **Kristian Hla Larte Chanchin** (Christian Popular Hymns)—1992, **Theihnghilh Ni Hlawm Suh Se** (Not To Be Forgotten)—1991, **Zoram-Thim Ata Engah** (Mizoram from Darkness to Light)—1988, **Pum Titi** (Common Gossip)—1985, **Zorama Kristian Hmasate Tihduhdahna** (Persecution of Early Mizo

Christians)—1985, **Zoram Zirna Lam Chhinchhiahna** (History of Mizoram Education)—1979, **Matric Arithmetic for Cl. VII-X** (Mathematics-Cl.-VII-X)—1957.

Contact Information

Lalhmuaka
Mamre
Macdonald Hill,
Zarkawt, P.O. : Aizawl-796007,
Telephone : 0386-2342173

CAPTAIN L. Z. SAILO

Personal

L.Z. Sailo was born on November 21, 1924, in Sialhawk village. His father was the Mizo Chief Liankanglova. Sailo joined the Indian Army during World War II at an early age on November 21, 1941. He was selected to join the UNO Peace Keeping Force and was sent to Congo, Africa where French was the common language. He was promoted to Captain in 1960, while he was still in Africa. During his tenure of service he had the opportunity to visit many countries of the world and work with the Red Cross Society in Geneva.

After years of military service in the UNO Peace Keeping Force, he retired on February 14, 1972. After retirement from service, he was engaged as a social worker at Dr. Graham's Home, Kalimpong from 1972 to 1974.

Since 1992 he has been the Home Father of Gamnuam Home, Churachandpurm, Manipur, where drug addicts are looked after. As a retired Captain, he has rendered invaluable service to this Home, especially during disturbances in Manipur.

He is now living in Churachandpur, Manipur with his wife, Ngurthanzuali Sailo, and five children.

In his area a coordination committee was formed by representatives of ten villages so that disputes among them may be settled amicably. Sailo was elected Chairman.

On the 61st Anniversary of the Nuptial Celebration on December 12, 2000, Sailo was privileged to be the Chief Guest and he was given a memento in honour of his outstanding social service.

Education

While in military service, he continued his education and he successfully passed Intermediate Science. He opted for French in college. Soon after college he obtained his Intermediate Science degree, he was promoted to the post of Viceroy Commission Officer.

Contributions

Sailo is a well-known writer. He has written more than thirty books so far, out of which ten books have already been published. He has composed more than three hundred and fifty songs and poems, and he is known among the Mizos as a renowned poet.

He has served as the President of the Zo Re-Unification Organisation during 1981-1999 in the state of Manipur, where communal consciousness is highly developed. He was given the **Gaidinlu Award** by the ZORO headquarters in 2000 for untiringly working for unification for eighteen years at his own expense. His fervent desire for communal harmony is deeply felt throughout Mizoram and its neighbouring states.

When the Paite clan and the Kuki clan clashed over communal differences, the government of Manipur launched a Communal Harmony Programme and L.Z. Sailo was one of the invitees who delivered a speech at Gandhi Memorial Hall, Imphal. In addition to his speech he also composed as many as twelve poems to promote communal harmony. These songs were sung by artists to instill the spirit of harmony in the hearts of the people.

He is a recipient of **Lelte Magazine's Lifetime Achievement Award** for his meritorious services. His valuable contributions are recognised and appreciated by many NGOs. **Certificates of Appreciation** have been awarded to him by Thingkangphai YMA (Young Mizo Association), Group YMA, Joint YMA, and the Mizo Literature Society.

One of his books entitled **Runlum Nuthai** was declared **Book of the Year-2002** by the Mizo Academy of Letters.

Selected Published Works

Awi Karel Lucknow-II (Oh Lucknow!-II story based on a soldier's life)—2003, **Hman Lai An Chang Zo Ta** (Days Gone by)—2002, **Runlum Nuthai** (Perfect House wife)—2002, **Suihlunglen Hlahril** (Sentimental Poems)—2001, **Thilmak Chhuisen Loh** (My serious object)—1999, **Awmkhawhar Suilunglen** (Love-Sick)—1998, **Awl Karel Lucknow** !-I (Oh Lucknow!-I)—1997, **Mizo Hnam Dan Thu**

Leh Hla (Mizo Customs and Ceremonies)—1991, **Thanghniangi Leh Rualkhuma** (Thanghniangi and Rualkhuma)—1991, **Hmangaihna tluantling** (True Love)—1938, **Nghilhoh par** (Unforgettable Sweetheart).

Un-published Works

Zoeate Mizia (Mizo Temperament), **Kohhran Thlanghem Chanchin** (History of Indigenous Cults), **Pi Pu Sulhnu** (Footprints of the Ancestors), **Zoro** (Zo Reorganisation), **Eiseina Nen** (With Hope), **Sakhaw Hrang Hrang Chanchin** (History of Religions), **German Ral Run** (War with Germany)–1917, **Tute Nge Kan Nih?** (Who are We?), **Rinawmna** (Honesty), **Khawvel Indopui Painihna** (Second World War), **Juda Hnam Chanchin** (History of the Jews), **Khawvel Sakhaw Chanchin** (ENG) (History of World Religions), **Wilow par Nih ?** (Willow), **Ka Fan Vei Ram** (Countries I Have Visited), **Hranghlutte Suhinu** (Footprints of the Braves), **Mizoram Fanna** (Tour within Mizoram), **Ringla Ring Suhla** (Believe it or not), **Mizoram Buai Chanchin** (Disturbance in Mizoram), **Rose Par Vul Ve Ta Lo Chu (In Press)** (An Un-bloomed Maiden). **Relthang Ka Dawn Zo Lo (In Press)** (I Don't Care What People Say).

Contact Information

Capton L.Z. Sailo
C/o Lengchhawn Press
Khatla, Aizawl-796001
Mizoram

LALRAMMAWIA NGENTE

Personal

Lalrammawia Ngente was born on June 21, 1968. His father's name is Thanmawia. He works as a lecturer in Johnson College Language Department.

Education

B.A. Harangdana College, Aizawl, M.A. in Public Administration from NEHU, Shillong. **Contributions**

Ngente has written about two hundred essays on various topics which have been published in different journals and magazines. He has been primarily interested in the promotion and enrichment of Mizo literature. Many of his essays and articles also deal with social reforms. He is a member of many groups including the Mizo Academy of Letters, Mizo Literature Forum, Zo-Poet-Playwright-Essayist-Novelist and the Mizo Language and Literature Teacher Association.

Presently he is serving as Joint Secretary of **Sabereka Khuangkaih**, a monthly literature Journal published in Aizawl. He has also been writing papers and organising seminars from time to time. **Select**

Published Works

Inhnialna Ropui (Great Controversy)—2004, **Dam Lai Thlan Thim** (Miserable Life)—2003, **Hringnun Hlimthla** (Collection of Essays)—2003, **Krista Pasalthate Nupa Nun Ngaihnawm** (Christian Couple)—2000, **Thim Lal Kohhran** (Satanic Church)—2000, **Biakzinna**-II (Pilgrimage-II)—1998, **Biakzinna-I** (Pillgrimage-I)—1997, **Khawvel Nghawringtu Television** (Television World-Wide-Media)—1994, **Mi Ropuite Hringnun** (Lives of Great Men)—1987.

Contact Information

Lalrammawia Ngente
Luangmual Vengtlang
P.O. : Aizawl-796012,
Mizoram
Telephone : 0389-2345730

NUCHHUNGI RENTHLEI

Personal

Nuchhungi Renthlei was born in 1914. Her father's name was Hmingliana, and her husband was R.Rualkhuma. She has one son and five daughters, and she is a retired teacher.

Education

Renthlei passed Middle English from the Baptist Missionary Society, Langlui (Mizoram).

Contributions

Smt. Nuchhungi Renthlei, a poetess, has composed seventy-two songs. She has also composed a number of cradle songs, rhymes, and responsive songs. She also currently has eighty-two poems in press. She herself was a popular singer in her younger days. Later, she became a music teacher in the school and taught both music, practice and theory.

Renthlei started writing fictional stories when she was a child. After becoming a teacher, she spent a lot of time on writing books for school children, as well as stories for adults.

She has contributed much to the preservation of Mizo culture through her poems. She also taught children traditional Mizo dances. Even after her retirement, she responded to the call of young Mizos. She developed an association and cultural society to teach students traditional dances.

Renthlei also started the **Girls' Auxiliary** in 1939 and strived hard for women's liberation even before many other parts of the world were aware of the concept.

She was the **Padma Shree** recipient in the field of literature in 1986. In addition to this, she has been awarded a number of certificates of honour and appreciation from several different forums.

Selected Published Works

Poetry

Poems for Mizo children—1984, Cradle Songs—1982.

Textbooks

Savawm Pathum (Three Bears)—1972, Khawvel Naupangte (Children of the World)—1967, Mizo Children and Games—1965, Little Indian Boy—1965, Zirna Bulbu (Primer)—1965, Serkawn Graded Reader-I—1938, Serkawn Graded Reader-II—1938, Serkawn Graded (Graded) Reader-III—1938.

Contact Information

Nuchhungi Renthlei
Serkawn, P.O. : Zotlang-796691,
District : Lunglei,
Mizoram
Telephone : 0372-2342134

R. THUNGVUNGA

Personal

R. Thangvunga is a Mizo writer. He was born on January 1, 1952 at Vanghmun in Zampui Hill of Tripura. His father was R. Thangluaia. Presently he is in Government Aizawl College, Aizawl.

Education

Thangvunga did his B.A.(Hons) and M.A. from Gauhati University. He obtained his Ph.D. from N.E. Hills University.

Contribution

R. Thungvunga translated **Twelfth Night**, the famous drama of Shakespeare into Mizo language. He also prepared some papers for seminars as well.

Selected Published Works

Twelth Night (Translation of Shakpeare's Drama in Mizo).

Contact Information

Kanan, Aizawl
Telephone : 0382-2340359

R.L. THANMAWIA

Personal

R. L. Thanmawia was born on September 20, 1954. His parents were late Vanlalliana. He works as a Reader in the Mizo Department of Mizoram University. He participated in many Developmental and Voluntary Bodies (Present office only). He is Secretary of Aizawl North Presbytery, Mizoram Synod (Church).

Education

Matriculation (HSLC) in 1975 from Kawrthah High School, Mizoram, P. U. and B.A in 1979 from Aizawl College, Aizawl, M.A. in 1981 from NEHU, Shillong, Ph.D. on Mizo Poetry in 1989 from NEHU, Shillong.

Contributions

Thanmawia is a poet and playwright. His twelve books have been published, out of which three are books on poetry and one dictionary. He has also written three plays and many articles. Besides these he has published twenty poems and is waiting to publish several more. He also has four plays which are still unpublished.

He has also edited **Thulehhla,** an official organ of the literary Journal of the Mizo Academy of Letters for twelve years. He was also on the Editorial Board of Journals and Magazines, viz. **Kum Za Lamtluang** (Published by Mizo Academy of Letters), **Kailawn Zo Kalsiam and Kristiath Thalai Kailawn** was published by the Mizo Writers Association.

Dr. Thanmawia serves currently as secretary of the Mizo Academy of Letters. He is also a member of the Advisory Board, Tribal Arts and Culture and Language, the Mizoram Publication Board, the Governing Board, North East Zone Cultural Centre, the Expert Committee on Mizo Language, CBSE, the Expert Committee on Mizo Language, SCERT, the Board of Studies, Mizoram University, and the Mizo-Writers Association.

Selected Published Works

Junior Zirlai Bu-I and II (Junior Lessons-I&II)—2002-03, **Mizo Poetry** (Mizo Poetry)—1998, **Senmei** (Collection of Poems)—1997, **Zinkawng Rapthlak Zawhtute** (Mizo Blind Poets)—1994, **Zofate Rohlu** (Mizo Poets and Their Poetry)—1992, **Dictionary of Mizo Poetic Terms** (Dictionary of Mizo Poetic Terms)—1988, **Chuailo** (Fadeless)—1987, **Ka Tai Pek Che Kha** (A Necklace Which I Gave You)—1987, **Naupangte Thian** (Friend of Children)—1987.

Booklets

Rinawmna (Honesty)—2002, **Ch. Pasena Chanchin** (Biography of Pasena)—2002, **Hun Hman Dan** (Utility of Time)—1989.

Editoral of Journal & Books

Editor, **Thu leh Hla**, (A literary Journal)—1988-2000, Published by Mizo Academy of Letters 12 years, **A member of Editorial Board, Kum Za Lamtluang**.—published by Mizo Academy of Letters, **Zo Kaksiam**–published by Mizo Academy of Letters, **Kailawn**–published by Mizo Writers Association, **Kristian Thalai**, published by Central KTP.

Aticles/Essays/Papers

Mizo	:	Hundred (more than)
English	:	Ten (ten)
Poetry published	:	Twenty (poems)
Unpublished	:	Ten (poems)
Play Unpublshed	:	Four

Contact Information

R.L. Thanmawia
Din Din Heaven
Ramhlun South, P.O. : Aizawl-796012
Mizoram
Telephone : 0389-2340128

Nagaland

Tenydie

NEICHURIAZO CHUCHA

Personal

Neichuriazo Chucha was born in 1948 at Khonoma village of Kohima District, Nagaland. His parents, who belonged to Angami Naga Tribe, were very poor and illiterate farmers. After matriculation he joined the government middle school in Khonoma as a teacher and was later promoted and transferred to the Government High School, Kohima, as language teacher. He was appointed as a lecturer at Kohima Science College, Jotsoma in 1993.

Education

Although he joined primary school in 1954, he could finish his middle school education only in 1963, due to political disturbances in Nagaland. He pursued his graduation (1984) and post graduation (1988) from Ura University.

Contributions

Along with some colleagues, Chucha has undertaken extensive research on the origin of Naga people and the similarities in their culture and language to the Chinese and Burmese. He has found certain striking similarities between these cultures.He has been writing articles and papers on the culture and language of the Naga people. Many of these have been published in magazines and journals.

He is also a recipient of the **State of Nagaland Award for Teachers** (1999) and **National Award for Teachers** (1996) in recognition of valuable services to the community as a teacher of outstanding merit.

Contact Information

Neichuriazo Chucha
House No. 17
Kohima Science College campus,
P.O. Science College,
Kohima-797002 Nagaland
Telephone : 0370-2223849

R. VASHUM

Personal

R. Vashum was born on January 3, 1969. He is involved in the cause of the indigenous people and the marginalized sections of the society.

Education

Vashum is a graduate of Imphal and Manipur University. He obtained his Master's in Social Anthropology in 1994 from Delhi University. He received a Doctor of Philosophy in Social Anthropology from Delhi University in 1999. The theme of his doctoral thesis is **Self-rule and people's assertion.** He completed his post-doctoral research on possible resolutions of the India-Naga conflict under the aegis of the Indian Social Institute, New Delhi. He presently works with the Developing Countries Research Centre, University of Delhi.

Contributions

Vashum explains–**The area of my research, academic training, and specialization and other extra-curricular activities and involvement are wide-ranging and are multi-disciplinary in nature. But largely, they revolve around the issues of welfare, dignity and rights of human societies, particularly of the marginalized and weaker sections of society. Some of these broad themes include aspects of state, governance, development, identity, civil society, people's unrest and dissents (including social movements), human rights violations and conflict resolution.**

He is engaged in dissemination of his findings in the form of articles and publications (books and journals). Along with some other scholars, writers and social activists, he launched a biannual journal, the **Naga Journal of Indigenous Affairs** in 2001 to help identify and address the issues of the indigenous and tribal people as well as gender issues.

Selected Published Works

Nagas : **Right to Self-Determination : An Anthropological-Historical Perspective**—2000, **Indo-Naga Conflict: Problem and Resolution** (New Delhi: Indian Social Institute)—2000, **Co-edited, State, Development and Identity in South Asia: a Search for Alternative Paradigms Ed. R. Vashum and Prakash Louis** (New Delhi: Indian Social Institute), **Co-edited, Extraordinary Laws in India: A Reader for Understanding Legislations Endangering Civil Liberties** (New Delhi: Indian Social Institute)—2002, **Co-edited, Nagas at Work**—1996.

Contact Information

R. Vasum
Developing Countries Research Centre
University of Delhi, Moris Nagar,
opposite Rangas Cottage, New Delhi-110007
Telephone: 011-2766-6281
E-mail: reivashum@hotmail.com

REV. DR. V.K. NUH

Personal

The Reverend Dr. V.K. Nuh (born 1935) is the General Secretary of the Council of Naga Baptist Churches in Nagaland, North East India. Beginning his unique mission at the age of twenty, he has established himself as a prominent Naga leader. In his earlier days, he served as an evangelist in the Chakhesang Baptist Church Council and later on became the Chaplain in the Naga Army. .During his Chaplainship, he was incarcerated as a political prisoner in the Imphal Central Jail but this did nothing to dampen his enthusiasm. His vision to minister to the Nagas was in fact expanding, and taking him to unexplored territories.

Eventually, Dr. V.K. Nuh began to serve as a headmaster in a Bible School and then went on to become the Pastor of Chizami Baptist Church. His precious contributions to his society did not go unrecognized. He was later ordained as a Baptist Minister, and it was at this juncture that the evolution and maturity of his Christian Mission found stable ground. He then served as the Field Director of Chakhesang Baptist Church Council from 1971 to 1992. During his tenure he was instrumental in bringing about many social changes in the land, from establishing schools, seminaries, and churches to initiating rural developmental programmes and missionary enterprises.

In due course, he emerged as a vital spokesperson in a society characterized by socio-political upheaval. Today he is best recognized as a man who struggles for peace and justice in Nagaland.

He has served variously as Member of the Consultative Body, **Nagaland Peace Mission** by Nagaland Baptist Church Council—1964-70, President, Nagaland Peace Council by Nagaland Baptist Church Council—1988-95, Chairman, Peace Commission by Council of Naga Baptist Churches—1995-2000, Participated in Conflict Resolution at Atlanta, USA—1997, Convener Peace and Justice Committee, Evangelical Fellowship of India—1985, Co-Chairman Intensive Training, Conflict Resolution of Asia, Bangkok—1995, and Member of Goodwill Mission, Neighboring States—2000.

The accomplishments of Rev. Dr. Nuh have been as various and colourful as the man himself. Decades of experience coupled with efforts to update his Theological Studies have made him an outstanding contributor to society. He hails from a humble background and has suffered hardships of life along with his people. The man, the vision and his genuine love for his motherland are truly geared toward fulfilling what he views as his special calling from God.

Education

Rev. Dr. V.K. Nuh started his pre-primary school in the village under Pastor Tsozu in 1942 and did primary schooling at Kohima Mission School in 1944. In that same year he left the school because the Second World War was fought in part at Kohima. After the war, he joined the first middle school that was opened in 1945 at Pfutsero and completed by 1950. Thereafter, he did his schooling at Ukhrul and Kohima. His first Theological education was at the Bible Institute Jorhat Assam (now known as Eastern Theological College) in 1959. Subsequently, he joined the Calcutta Bible College (1961-63) from which he obtained a Diploma in Theology. Later, he did two months study at the Golden Gate Baptist Theological Seminary, San Francisco, USA.

Contributions

He has written twenty-two books which provide not only authentic information about the ongoing Naga socio-political struggle but also reveal the violations of human rights among an oppressed group of indigenous people. Besides this, Rev. Nuh has presented more than 100 resource papers at state, national and international levels.

In his extensive travels,both within the country and abroad, he has acted as a reliable representative figure of the Nagas. On such occasions the issues presented for open dialogue have always focused on Conflict Resolution, Indigenous People's Struggles, Human Right Studies and Peace-Making Initiatives.

He received many Awards of out of which some are mentioned here. Distinguished **Leadership Award,** American Biographical Institute Inc.—1997, **Great Achievers of India,** Front for National

Progress, Delhi—2001, **Best Citizens of India**, International Friendship Society—2003, **National Prabha Gold Medal**, Integrated Council of Socio-Economic Progress New Delhi—2003, Master of Divinity Degree Thesis for **Rev. Dr. V. K. Nuh : His Contribution Towards The Naga Society**, Submitted to the Federated Theological Programme of North East India—2003 by Seyievino Medeo—2003.

In recognition of his lifetime works, he was conferred an Honorary title of Emeritus, and made Executive Secretary by the Chakhesang Baptist Church Council on December 6th, 1992. Consequently, he was awarded an Honorary Doctorate of Divinity at Gurukul Theological Seminary, Madras, on July 20th, 1993.

Selected Published Works

When the Battle is Over, Kohima, CNBC—2004, **Utsiepfumia Mhasi Bode**, Ura Academy, Kohima—2004, **In Search of Praxis Theology for the Nagas**, Regency Publications, New Delhi—2003, **The Naga Chronicle**, Regency Publications New Delhi—2002, **Struggle for Indentity in North East India**, Spectrum Publications, New Delhi—2001, **My Native Country**, New Delhi—2001, **Crusade on Naga Morality**, Key Data Processing Calcuttas—2000, **Theological Reflection on Naga Society**, Key Data Processing, Calcutta—2000, **Participation in Suffering and Struggle**, ISPCK, Delhi—1997, **Episode of Naga Tragedy**, Printwell, Dimapur—1995, **Revive Us Again**, Evangelical Literature Depot, Calcutta—1995, **Efforts Towards Naga Unity**, Kohima Key Data, Calcutta—1993, **My Country My People**, Vision Press, Kohima—1988, **Nagaland Church and Politics**, Vision Press, Kohima—1986. **Mother's Love**, Citizen Press, Kohima—1971

Contact Information

Rev. Dr. V.K. Nuh
Genral Secratery, Council of Naga Baptist Church,
Post Box 275, City : Kohima,
Dist. : Kohima,
Nagaland -7970011

KEKHRIEVOU YHOME

Personal

Kekhrievou Yhome was born on April 17, 1970 into a poor farming family in L. Khel Kohima village. She is the eldest daughter of the late Suolaie Yhome and Neilieu Yhome. Her father passed away when she was in class nine. Soon after her father's death, her mother's health became worse, and the family responsibility fell on Yhome's shoulders. Before her class 10 results, she got a Government job, and she had this responsibility along with caring for her ailing mother and three younger brothers and three younger sisters. With that income she supported her family and brought up her brothers and sisters. But after some years her job was terminated by the department.

Education

Due to her family problems she had to struggle hard to complete her studies, even up to class ten. Currently she is continuing her studies from IGNOU at Kohima.

Contributions

Yhome says—**To be a writer is like a dream for me. I came to know that this is a gift from God.** Her first novel was **Azo Kekhrie Menguyalie** which means **Longing for My Mothers Love.** This novel was also translated into English, which she is planning to publish soon. One of her novels, **Kedietho capiu**, published in 2000, is used as a textbook in Pre-University. Her goal is to become the first women novelist in Tunyidie language of Nagaland. Fifty nine poems in Tunyidie have been published in **Ura Dze**, a monthly literary Journal of Ura Academy Kohima, and eighteen poems were included in the book of **Tenyimia Mhaphru** published by Ura Academy. This book is also being used as a college textbook. She is also planning ultimately to translate all of her books into English.

Selected Published Works

A Nei Ketho Zo Part-II (Novel)—2004, **A Nei Ketho Zo Part-I** (Novel)—2003, **Jihova n khrieya** (Novel)—2003 (Translated from English into Tenyidie), **Tsie We Siliete** (Novel)—2002, **Kiju Nu Su Tseite** (Novel)—2000, **Kedietho Capiu** (Novel, B.A. Text book)—2000, **Azuo Kekhrie Menguyalieh** (Novels)—1999.

Contact Information

Kekhrievou Yhome
Village : L. Khel Kohima
P.O.Box-392, Distt. : Kohima-797001
State-Nagaland
Telephone : 0370-2270515

Tripura
Kokborok

CHANDRA KANTA MURASINGH

Personal

Chandra Kanta Murasingh was born at Twiwandal, Tripura on April 1, 1957. His father is Shyampada Murasigh and Mother is Laxmi Devi. Chandra Kanta Murasingh is presently employed in a bank.

Contribution

Chandra Kanta Murasingh is an eminent poet of Tripura and has six published Poetry books to his credit. Translated version of his selected poems has also been published. Besides these his two Anthologies have also been published.

Besides creative writing, he is actively associated in different capacities with various literary and cultural societies and institutions of Tripura viz., Secretary, Kokbrok Sahitya Academy (NGO), Agartala, member, Governing Body of E.Z.C.C., Kolkata, Member, Tripura State Kala Academy, Member, Tripura Cultural Advisory Board, Government of Tripura, Member, Tribal Cultural Research Institute, Government of Tripura.

He received the **Sahitya Academy Bhasha Samman Award**, 1996. For his outstanding contribution to poetry he also received two state level awards **Mahendra Debbarma Memorial Award** (1996) and **Rabindra Smriti Puraskar** (2001).

Published Works

Poetry

Lok Chethuwang Lok (Rise up Chethuwang tree)—1999, **Holong Kok Sao Bolong Bisingo**(The stone speaks in the forset)—1995, **Haping Garingo Chibuksa Ringo**—(The pithon calls the deserted Tong house)—1987, **Pindi Walwi Pin**(Spread the rain), **Ruphaini Buduk Ani Nogo** (The Silver rope in my room), **Deng Deng Bachagwra** , **Select Poems** (Translated).

Anthologies

Bolong Kwkhwrang Fehelkha Bwkwrang (The green forset moves)—1987, Kolomtwi Kisi Mwkhang (Sweating)—1986.

Contact Information

Chandra Kanta Murasingh
New Model Village
PO: Abhoynagar- 799005 Distt: Tripura (W)
Telephone: 0381- 231-1177®, 222-6502
Fax : 0381-2310150
E-mail: murasingh@rediffmail.com

BIMAL DEB BARMA

Personal

Bimal Deb Barma was born on January 8, 1971 in Ampura, Tripura. He is a member of the Tripuri tribe. When he was a student of class one, he made a statue of Rama out of clay. He became expert in making statues of Durga and Kali. He is considered to be a good dancer and performed the Munda stick dance and other tribal dances like the Garia dance.

Education

Barma has completed his Madhyamik education. He studied from 1st class to 5th class between 1977 and 1987 in Fulgama Choudhury Junior Basic School and studied from class 6 to class 10 at Ampura High School from 1985 to 1991. He wrote his Madhymik examination at Chebri Higher Secondary School in 1991.

Contributions

He is a poet, novelist, short story writer, drama writer, singer, songwriter, filmmaker and image maker. Using the Bengali script, he writes mainly in the Kokborok language, focusing on tribal culture. All his books are published by Kokbrok Sahitya Samsad, Agartala, Tripura.

He formed a Cultural team Named **Sandok Chilpi Bodal** (Tribal Cultural Society). This team performed dramas along with **Jhum** Dance, **Goria** Dance and Folk Songs. He is directing another film called **Sayanda in Suwari** (Sayanda is a Musical Instrument of tribals, Suwari means disciple). A Film about the Kokborok Language named **Lama Duwari**, directed by him was released on April 18th, 2003. He also braughtb out a Magazine named **Kok Lame** in Kokbrok in the year 1991.

He received the following Awards from Directorate of IGAT Agartala, Gandhighat, Tripura, such as—**Chandrakanta Mura Singh, Rabindra Kishor Deb Berma, Sudhyan Tripura, Sunil Deb Barma,**

Nanda Kumar Deb Barma, Bikashray Deb Barma, Haripadya Deb Barma, Kunjabihari Deb Berma, Gito Ring, Hemanta Kumar Jamatia, Nakhury Jamatia, Shamalal Deb Barma, Nagandra Jamatia.

Selected Published Works

Muithuni sal (The day of remembrance)—2001, **Khuchug Hachikam** (A Story of Tripura, a poem)—2001, **Singsong** (The bird inside the cage, This book of poetry includes 30 of Deb's Poems—2000, **Twisha Lamjar** (The way of stream)—1998, **Shachalang Jorani Emamgni Kumpui** (The Dream of Kumpui, Kumpui is the name of a Flower of the spring season)—1995, **Janni Maya** (Mercy for my life)—1993, **Khepal Kathama** (The story of life. This was staged at many places in Tripura)—1990.

Contact Information

Bimal Deb Barma
Ampura, Bharat Sardarpar, West District
Tripura-799207
Telephone : 03825-224247

BINOY DEBBARMA

Personal

Binoy Debbarma was born in a peasant family on January 27, 1963 in Hurunia Chokdiri Kamu in West Tripura. His father, the late Gonadhan Debbarma, was of the Borok (Tripuri) tribe. His mother was the late Sajani Debbarma.

Education

Binoy Debbarma is a university graduate.

Contribution

Binoy Debbarma has written poems, short stories and criticism. He has also edited some literary magazines. In addition to poetry, fiction and criticism, he has written a **History of Tripura**, a book of Kokborok grammar, and compiled a **Kokborok-English-Bengali Dictionary**. He has also prepared coursebooks for primary school educators.

Selected Published Works

Anglo-Kokborok-Bengali Dictionary—2002, **Yamroksa** (Kokborok Folktale)—2002, **Concise Kokborok-English-Bengali Dictionary** (Language Cell Education Department)—2001, **Twipra Bisi and Borok Jati** (about Tripura history and people)—1999, **Sonnet Koktangrok** (sonnet poems)—1998, **1409 Tring** (about Tripura Era)—1999, **Phumukmung** (Kokborok riddles)—1994, **Kokborokni Rangchak-Richak** (Ornamental terms of Kokborok)—1994, **Kokborok Kokma** (Kokborok Grammar)—1994, **Nakhrai** (short stories)—1989.

Contact Information

Binoy Debbarma
Ujan Abhoynagar, Near Model School
Agartala –799005 (Tripura)
Telephone: 0381-2346079 / 2347235

MILAN RANI JANATIA

Personal

Milan Rani Janatia was born on June 5, 1976, in Meghalaya. She is a member of the Janatia Tribe. She works as a research scholar (Junior Research Fellow) at North Eastern Hill University, Meghalaya.

Education

Janatia is a postgraduate.

Contribution

Janatia writes short stories and poems in the Kokborok language and in Hindi.

Contact Information

Milan Rani Janatia
Shillong, P.O. : Permanent, NEHU Campus,
East Khasi Hill District,
Meghalaya, Pin-793022
Telphone : 551747 (Bilgito Hostel, NEHU)

NANDA KUMAR DEBBARMA

Personal

Debbarma was born on December 11, 1951 in Tripura. Currently a member of the Tripura Legislative Assembly, Agartala.

Education

He studied in his village and M.B.B. College Agartala.

Contributions

Debbarma writes in both Kokborok and Bengali. He has also a composer and director of dramas. He has several books and dramas in Kokborok to his credit. He has published thirteen books to date. He is also a dramatist, having performed both drama and music on All India Radio and Doordarshan and other places. He has also presented poems at National and International literary and Cultural Festivals.

He has directed several serials on Doordarshan, and has represented the state ofTripura in several regional and national cultural festivals.

He is a judge for the Akasvani Audition Board and conducts public music lessons on All India Radio.

He has received prizes from **Eklabya Sahitya**, the International Geeta Society, and the Tripura Tribal Areas Autonomous District Council. He has also received the **Mahendra Smriti for Drama** and the **Rabindra Puraskar.**

Selected Published Works

Kokborok Poetry

Simalwng Sakao Hologni Khum (Stone Flowers in Burnial Place), **Bologni Bwsagursong Mwsao** (Dances of Jungle Girls), **Ani Ganao Ang** (Me beside me), **Dugmalino** (To a Flower).

Bengali Poetry

Alo, Saboa, Padatic, Sakharne Nabanna, Ekada Mukhegita Aranye, Bane Badare, Thikane Kirat Bhumi.

Kokborok Novel

Rung (The Boat).

Kokborok Drama

Kokkisa Kaktang Hai, Mari, Whal Swbaina Imang, Imangni Bwsank, Sikhok, Raondijwkma, Bolongni Mukharwi Swral, Rig Sunam, Koktan Khitai Bai, Nuai, Kwpwlai, Suehi Bakhaukswk, Durg, Dogar, Longlore me Wkobza, Swkagu Choba Kotar, Chobar Kharang, Laugnani Kochujuk.

Translation into Kokborok

Gita, Mahabharata for Children, Bratiya Roiner katha (Poems by A. Sarkar).

Contact Information

Nanda Kumar Debbarma
Tripura Legislative Assembly
P.O. : Agartala-799001
Telephone : (0381) 232-1982 (R), 9436124454 (M)

SUNIL DEB BARMA

Personal

Sunil Deb Barma was born on January 25, 1958 at Herma village, situated in Bishalgarh, Tripura West. His father was the late Jatindra Deb Barma and mother late Jashuda Deb Barma.

Education

Higher Secondary

Contribution

Sunil Deb Barma is a multi-faceted literary figure and writes short stories, poems and novels. He has edited some books too. He has also compiled a trilingual dictionary of Bengali, Kokborok and English. He is a recipient of the **Salil Krishna Debbarman Memorial Award, 2001**. He is presently Secretary of the Kokborok Sahitya Samsad, a tribal cultural and literary organization.

Selected Published Works

Poetry

Risa—2000.

Short Stories

Busu—1999, Bolongni Khum—1996.

Novels

Langmani Rukungo—2001.

Dictionary

Tribhasha Sabdwamala—2001.

Edited Books

Jora, Khumnulwng.

Jointly Edited Book

Anji.

Contact Information

East New Palli, Krishnanagar
Agartala, Tripura West

BODHRAI DEBBARMA

Personal

Bodhrai Debbarma was born on December 20, 1956 at Chargharıya, Mendui in Tripura. His father was the late Dayal Chandra Debbarma, Bodhrai Debbarma is a teacher by profession. He has been active in social work and previously served as a legislator in Tripura assembly representing the CPI (M).

Education

M.A. B.Ed.

Contribution

Bodhrai writes poetry and essays. Being a social activist in his essays, he focuses predominantly on the problems of the Kokborok. He has to his credit two published poetry collections. He is the recipient of the **Sudhanwa Debbarma Sahitya Puraskar** for 2003.

Selected Published Works

Kolomtwi (Poetry), **Sal Manwa Sakang** (Poetry)

Contact Information

Kunjaben Township Quarter Complex
Type- II/83, PO: Kunjaben
Agartala
Phone: 0381- 2350481

RABINDRA KISHORE DEBBARMA

Personal

Rabindra Kishore was born on September 15, 1954 at a village called Kambukchhara in Tripura. His father late Krishna was a farmer. Rabindra Kishore Debbarma, however, chose teaching as his profession. He was the Executive Member (Health) of TTAADC from 1985 to 1990.

Education

B.A.

Contribution

Rabindra Kishore writes poetry, short stories, essays, etc. He has translated Kalidas's Meghdoot in Kokborok. Besides, he has edited a book on the controversy about the Kokborok script. He received the highest state award the '**Rabindra Puraskar**' in 2003 for his outstanding contribution to Kokborok literature. He has also been awarded the prestigious **Salil Krishna Smriti Puraskar** for short stories.

Selected Published Works

Short Stories

Hachukni Muktwi (Tears of the Hills)—2002, **Kereng Kothoma** (Tales of Folk)—2002.

Translation

Meghdoot (Bengali to Kokborok)—1982.

Others

Kokborok Prabad Bakye Tipra Loka-Jivan—2000.

Edited Books

Kokborok Lipi Bitarka—2005.

Contact Information

Thakur Palli Road (Near TRTC Office)
Krishnanagar, Agartala, West Tripura
Ph: 0381-2314432

SABITA DEBBARMA

Personal

Sabita Debbarma was born on January 1, 1972. Her father is Lalit Mohan Debbarma and mother Rajmala Debbarma. She is a teacher in a Government school.

Education

B.A.

Contribution

Sabita Debbarma writes poetry in her mother tongue Kokborok and Bengali. She has compiled a book of rhyming and a poetry book. She has participated in poetry recitation programs on the All India Radio, Agartala and various poetry recitations and seminars.

Selected Published Works

Kadeng-Kadang-Kadong (a book of rhyming)

Contact Information

Present

Quarter No.11/58
Shyamali Bazar, Kunjaben
Agartala, West Tripura
Tele: 0381-2350320

Permanent

Chhato Surma, Kamalpur,
Dhalai, Tripura

SEFALI DEBBARMA

Personal

Sefali Debbarma was born on March 2, 1964 at Pattabil village situated in West Tripura. Though a house wife, she is also active in social work in which she receives considerably support from her husband Kusum Debbarma, who is a school teacher.

Education

She was educated at home (no school).

Contribution

Sefali Debbarma is an eminent Kokborok poet. She has published two books of poetry. She received the **Salil Krishna Smriti Puraskar, 2004** for her contribution to Kokbrok poetry. She participated in the Bangladesh Jatiya Kabita Utsav- 2004 held in Dhaka on an invitation received from the Bangladesh Jatiya Kabita Parishad.

Hor Diporo Rwchap wang (Song at Midnight), **Emangni Yakhrai Ninanggo** (Tremor of the bridge of dream)

Contact Information

New Model Village
(Near Sachin Debbarma Setu)
PO: Abhoynagar (Agartala)
Pin Code: 799005

SHYAMLAL DEBBARMA

Personal

Shyamlal Debbarma, the son of late Ramani Mohan Debbarma and Bratkanya Debbarma, was born on November 2, 1951 at Rangmala village which is situated in Bishalgarh Sub Division of West Tripura.

Education

B.A. (Political Science) from Tripura University.

Contribution

Shyamlal Debbarma writes in nearly all genres of literature, viz., poetry, drama, short stories, novels, essays etc. His articles appear in most important magazines and newspapers published in Kokborok language. He has published two short story collections, two poetry collections, three one act plays, two novels and three collections of rhyming. In addition, he also edited a few books of short stories and poems. He was also the editor of the Tripura Kagtoon, a weekly news bulletin published by Tripura Govt, for nearly seventeen years. He has also done some translation work. He was awarded the **Salil Krishna Debbarma Award—1998** and the **Rabindra Puraskar—2000**. Being an eminent poet of Tripura, he is almost invariably invited to poets' meet organized by the Govt of Tripura and the Tripura Tribal Areas Autonomous District Council.

In addition to writing in his mother tongue Kokborok, he is also associated with several cultural organizations in various capacities, such as Member, East Zone Cultural Center, Member, North-east Zone Cultural Center, President, Kokborok Sahitya Samsad, Jt Secretary, Tripura Samannay Kendra Executive Committee, Member, Tripura State Kala Academy, Member, Research Advisory Board, Govt of Tripura, Member, Cultural Advisory Committee, Govt of Tripura.

Selected Published Works

Poetry

Kokthairog Thwngo Bonbonia

Short Stories

Dundurkma, Choba Kaisani Ulo

Novels

Khong, Tongthai Naitugui

Rhyme Books

Kogtang Bwtang, Chingchong, Chingchong Maching Chong

SNEHAMOY ROY CHOWDHURI

Personal

Snehamoy Roy Chowdhuri was born on January 5, 1961 at Agartala, Tripura West. His father was the late Durgagati Roy Chowdhury and mother late Parul Roy Chowdhury.

Education

B.A.

Contribution

Snehamoy Roy Chowdhury is a poet, essayist and short story writer of eminence. He has published 5 collections of short stories and two of poetry. He has compiled a few books too. His articles have been published in several Kokborok newspapers and magazines. His writings have been included in the text books prescribed for secondary and higher secondary classes. He is a regular participant in various poetry recitation programs organized in and outside his state. He received in 1999 the prestigious **Salil Krishna Debbarman Memorial Award** for his outstanding contribution to Kokborok literature.

Besides literature, he has been actively participating in cultural activities. He is presently an Executive member (Treasurer) of the Kokborok Sahitya Parishad, a leading organization of tribal culture and literature in Tripura.

Selected Published Works

Poetry Collection

Mini Imangni hao—2001, Khwrangjak huk—1998.

Short Story Collection

Tangthakni Imang—2004, Chethuang talao—2000, Mazilatani Bwlawng—1999, Makal Bwskanga—1993.

Compiled Works

Kubaini Achai Gandhijy, Anji

Contact Information

Arundhutinagar, Rd. No.9, PO : A.D. Nagar, Agartala
Tripura West
Ph: 0381-2371549

Writers of Sikkim Living in West Bengal

Lepcha and Nepali

LYANGSONG TAMSANG

Personal

Lyangsong Tamsang was born on March 21, 1946 at Bom Bustee, Kalimpong in Darjeeling. He is the eldest son of K.P. Tamsang, a renowned Lepcha thinker, scholar, author and linguist. He is married and he has two sons. He is a member of the Advisory Committee Board, All India Radio, Kurseong. Tamsang is the General Secretary of the Indigenous Lepcha Tribal Association. He works for the conservation, preservation, maintenance, and development of the Lepcha language, literature, and cultural heritage. The Lepchas of West Bengal, under the leadership of Tamsang, are demanding for the introduction of the Lepcha language in schools and colleges in the Darjeeling district of West Bengal. This was introduced for Lepcha children in Sikkim in 1975, but so far has been ignored in West Bengal.

Education

Tamsang received his initial education at Kumudini Homes, Kalimpong.

Contributions

Tamsang has edited several magazines and books including **Aachuley**, a quarterly Lepcha bilingual magazine, and **King Gaeboo Achyok**, an annual Lepcha bilingual magazine. He has also opened thirty Lepcha night schools in remote villages in the Darjeeling District where Lepcha language and culture are taught to tribal children. He has also instituted the **K.P. Tamsang Lepcha Language and Literary Award** which is given annually to an individual or institution, irrespective of caste, creed, or nationality, who works for the maintenance and development of Lepcha language and literature.

For his contributions to the maintenance and preservation of Lepcha language and culture, Tamsang has been awarded the **Lok Bhasha Samman** (Gandhi Hindustani Sahitya Sabha) 2001, and **Vir**

Birsa Munda National Award (Akhil Bharatiya Adivasi Vikas Parishad) 2003.

Selected Published Works

Tribals and their Education (Gandhi Hindustani Sahitya Sabha, Delhi), **and A Collection of Tales about the Sikkim and Nepal Himalayas.**

Cotact Information

Lyangsong Tamsomg
Lepcha Boys Hostal, Lower,
Bombasti, Kalimpong-734301

R.P. LAMA

Personal

R.P. Lama was born on March 12, 1931 at Chilownedhura, Pankhabari in the district of Darjeeling. His father was Rajman Lama and mother Charimaya Lama. He served in the Government of West Bengal for thirty years. From 1953 to 1958, he was in the Agriculture Department. During this period, he edited monthly agricultural journal **Kheti-pati**. In 1958, he moved to the Department of Information of Cultural Affairs where he worked as Sub-Divisional Publicity Officer and the Officer-in-charge of Hill Cultural Unit till 1989. He also led Nepali cultural delegation on behalf of the Government of West Bengal to Nepal, Delhi and other states of India.

Education

R.P. Lama received his primary education at Longview T.E. Primary School, Pankhabari, his place of birth. After doing matriculation in 1950 from Pushparani Boys High School, Kurseong, he passed the B.A. examination from St. Joseph's College, Darjeeling. Finally, he obtained his M.A. degree from North Bengal University, Siliguri, Darjeeling.

Contribution

R.P. Lama is one of the most articulate spokesman of Nepali literature in the recent times. An essayist, poet, short-story writer, biographer, dramatist, folklorist and editor, Lama has written widely on Nepali culture and literature. Besides writing, he has been associated with several literary and social organisation and institutions in various capacities, viz. General Secretary, Nepali Sahitya Sammelan, Darjeeling, President, Nepali Sahitya Sammelan, Darjeeling, Convenor, Indian National Trust for Art and Cultural Heritage, Member, Nepali Advisory Board Sahitya Akademi, convenor, Language Advisory Committee for Nepali Bharatiya Jnanpith,

Member, Panel of Experts, Union Public Service Commission, Member, Indian Red Cross Society, Member, Indo-Mongolian Friendship Society, Bombay, Member, Himali Lekhak Manch, Gangtok, Director, National Workship for Nepali Sahitya Akademi (1991), etc. He has also participated in various seminars, conferences and literary projects, etc., of which remarkable are: India-Nepal writers conference, New Delhi, January 20-21, International Conference on Culture, Education and Ecology in New Delhi from 13-16 October, 1995, National Literary project 'Knit India through literature' etc. He is presently working on study of tribals and their festivals in the hgills of Darjeeling sponsored by the Department of Culture, Ministry of Human Resource Development, Government of India and also compiling an annotated bibliography of translations in India and Nepal.

He is a recipient of President's Silver Medal and a citation in 1961 for excellent works in census operations, **Sahitya Akademi Award** (1992) for the book **Indra Dhanush**, a collection of essays on hill folk culture.

Selected Published Works

Original Works

Smritima (collection of poems, essays and short stories)—1971, **Haamro Panchayat** (drama on Panchayat Raj)—1972, **Radio Wartaharu** (collection of radio talks)—1981, **Nepali Sahitya Sammelan ko Swarna Jayanti**—1982, **Kirti stambh** (life and works of eminent persons of India and abroad)—1987, **Reprint**-1995, **Pratidhwani** (Drama on the heroism of Gurkhas in the war front)—1989, **Indradhanush** (collection of essays on hill culture), **Sahitya Akademi ra Nepali Bhasa**—1995, etc.

Translation

Barsha dinko-Char (Samkalin Bharatiya Sahitya, Sahitya Akademi in Hindi), **Varsha Dinko Char** (Annual number of 'Matribhumi' in Malyalam), **Bharat ka Vir Balakharu** (National Book Trust, India, in Nepali), **Nepal Katha Sihar Kosh** (Hindi).

Edited Works

Kheti-Pati (monthly agricultural journal, Desh Bhakti ka Geetharu (two editions)—1965 and 1974, **Smarika** (two volumes of hill culture)—1967 and 1978, **Diyalo** (literary journal published by Nepali Sahitya Sammelan Darjeeling), **Dal Bahadur Giri Smriti Granth** (English and Nepali)—1987, **Patrika Darjeeling** (annual bulletin published by Indian National Trust for Art and Cultural Heritage, Darjeeling Regional Chapter since)—1990, **Rahul Sankrityayan Centenary Souvenir**—1994, **Bharatiya Nepali Sahitya Rastriyatako Sandarbhama** (Sahitya Akademi)—1994.

Contact Information

R.P. Lama
Windsor Lodge,
Pamphawati Gurungni Road,
Happy Valley Tea Estate,
PO : Darjeeling, West Bengal